BOOTLEGS, BLITZES and BOMBS

RADCLIFFE R. PHILLIPS

Illustrations by
David Tidswell

COLUMBUS BOOKS
LONDON

IN MEMORY

To the memory of one of my best and dearest friends IAN ELLIOT, whose life was tragically cut short in his prime. I will miss you very much: you were the brother I never had.

Text copyright © 1987 Radcliffe R. Phillips
Illustrations copyright © 1987 Columbus Books Limited

First published in Great Britain in 1987 by
Columbus Books Limited
19-23 Ludgate Hill, London EC4M 7PD

Designed by Val Hill

British Library Cataloguing in Publication Data
Phillips, Radcliffe R.
   Bootlegs, blitzes and bombs: the language
   and terminology of American football.
   1. Football——Dictionaries
   I. Title
   796.332′03′21   GV951

ISBN 0-86287-330-4

Typeset by Falcon Graphic Art Ltd
Wallington, Surrey

Printed and bound by The Guernsey Press,
Guernsey, Channel Islands

INTRODUCTION

In all the years I've been around the football scene, I have never ceased to be amazed at the colour and humour of its language and terminology. I've tried in vain to find publications which would explain some of it in more detail. Having been unable to find one, I did some research and decided to write one myself, and I've certainly had a lot of fun compiling this handbook of terms, some of which are in common usage, others of which are used by famous coaches and/or TV and radio commentators.

R.R.P.

A

ACE
A formation which uses only one runningback in the backfield and utilizes three receivers and a tightend.

ACROSS
A pass play in which the receiver runs downfield for 5-10 yards then cuts across the field diagonally to the middle.

AIR IT OUT
A long pass completion or attempted pass for big yardage.

ALL
The ultimate accolade for any player is to be All-something, e.g. All-American, All-Conference, All-Pro, All-State (and, for exceptional players such as the Chicago Bears' Walter Payton, All-World).

ALL CURL
A play that requires the tightend and wide receivers to run downfield and curl back towards the line of scrimmage.

ALLEY
The area between the inner hash mark and the numbers on the field which is unmarked is called 'the alley'.

ALLEY-OOPS
A pass which follows a high trajectory, over the head of the defender, in the hope that the receiver can get to it

first. This type of pass was first used in the 1950s by Y.A. Tittle and R.C. Owens, San Francisco 49ers. Owens, a former basketball player, had exceptional leaping ability and made some spectacular catches in his time. Also called a lofted pass.

ALL-PURPOSE BACK
Formerly known as the T-formation back, this is a runningback who runs very well with the ball, is a good receiver out of the backfield, is a good blocker and can throw a pass on occasion.

ALL-PURPOSE YARDS
Statistical measurement for a player who has run from the line of scrimmage, caught passes, return kicks and punts.

ALL THE LIGHTS AREN'T ON
Said of players who appear to lack intelligence.

ALL THE WAY
When the ballcarrier takes the ball right into the end zone he has gone 'all the way'.

ANGLE BLOCK
An offensive line manoeuvre which cuts off the defensive lineman to one side of the offensive lineman.

ANIMAL
A rough, tough sort of player who is well known for getting physical, even after the play has been blown dead. The LA Raiders regularly produce such players.

AREA BLOCK
See zone blocking.

ARMCHAIR QUARTERBACK
The television viewer, watching the game at home, who gets every play right, once it has been run, by second-guessing everything. Also called a grandstand quarterback or Monday-morning quarterback.

AUDIBLE

When the quarterback gets to the line of scrimmage he sets up behind the centre ready to take the snap. He looks over the defence. If it appears that the play he has called in the huddle is unlikely to work, or if he thinks another play will work better, he calls an 'audible', a series of commands which tells his teammates the play has changed. This can be in the form of a colour code, numbers or letters. Also called an automatic, or checking-off.

AUTOMATIC
See audible, check off.

B

BACK
Offensive or defensive players in the backfield behind the line of scrimmage.

BACKFIELD IN MOTION
A penalty called against one or more offensive backs who move towards the line of scrimmage before the ball has been snapped.

BACK JUDGE
A match official whose primary responsibility is to look after the receiver on his side of the field and any out-of-bounds infractions.

BACK-PEDAL
The action of the defensive back as he covers the potential pass receiver running downfield. As the receiver runs forward the defender back-pedals, the better to observe his charge.

BACKS (OFFENSIVE)
These are the quarterback, the halfback, the fullback, the slotback, the wingback, the flankerback, the upback and the aceback.

BACKS (DEFENSIVE)
These are the cornerback, the safety and the roverback.

BACK-UP MAN
The defensive player who takes up his position a few yards behind a teammate. Should his teammate miss a

tackle on the opponent, the back-up man makes it instead.

BACKWARD PASS

A pass thrown parallel to or backward from the line of scrimmage usually from the quarterback to a runningback. Also called a toss, shuffle pass or pitchout.

BAIT THE HOLE

A play action fake into the line of scrimmage intended to fool the defender and set him up for a trap block.

BALANCE

Ability to maintain equilibrium. A successful ballcarrier must be able to stay on his feet after initial contact in order to gain extra yards, which requires good balance.

BALANCED LINE

The normal offensive line set: a centre, a left and right guard, a left and right tackle, a tightend and a wide receiver.

BALANCED OFFENCE

In order for a team to be consistently successful, it must be able to move the ball up and down the field through the air by passing or on the ground by rushing.

BALL

The prolate spheroid, made of pebble grain leather (not pigskin as most people think) and weighing 14-15 ounces, which is at the heart of the game.

BALL CONTROL FOOTBALL

The ability of the team in possession to move the ball downfield by using short- and medium-range passes and a steady running game while using up time and running out the clock.

BALL HAWK

A defensive player who always seems to be around the football, making interceptions or recovering fumbles.

BASIC T

One of the oldest formations in football, in which four backs are aligned behind the centre: a quarterback, a fullback directly behind the quarterback and two halfbacks on either side of the fullback. Also called a T-formation or tight T.

BAT THE BALL AWAY

The action, by an offensive or defensive player or special team player, of striking or punching the ball while blocking a punt or kick.

BELLY

The action of the quarterback as he thrusts the ball or fakes the thrust of the ball into the runningback's belly.

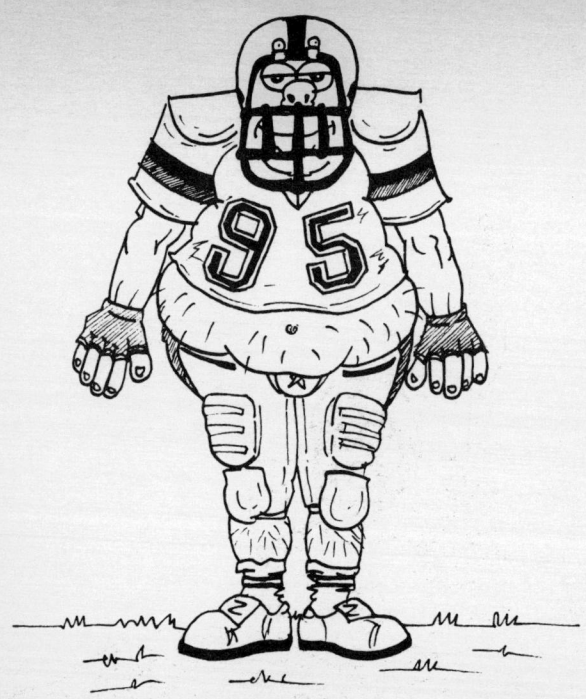

BELLY OUT
A pass pattern for a runningback who circles out of the backfield to make a catch, usually a screen pass.

BENCH
The area on the sideline between the two 30-yard lines where the players, coaches and team officials congregrate before and during the game. It is also the actual furniture on which the players sit.

BENCH-WARMER
A back-up player, reserve player or non-starter.

BIG PLAY GUY
A player who is expected to make a spectacular play by either catching a long pass, breaking a big run from the line of scrimmage, making a game-saving interception, causing or recovering a fumble or blocking a punt or field goal attempt.

BIRDCAGE
The rubber-covered metal tubing which is attached to a player's helmet to protect his face is also called a facemask or facecage.

BLACKOUT
In the US, if the National Football League's home team does not sell all the tickets for a game, there is an automatic television blackout for a 90-mile radius from the game.

BLACKSMITH'S ARM
A quarterback with a particularly strong throwing arm. Also called a rifle arm.

BLANKET COVERAGE
Pass coverage by defensive backs and linebackers where every potential receiver is covered as he comes out of the backfield or off the line of scrimmage.

16

BLAST
A straight-ahead power running play. Also called a dive.

BLIND SIDE
To block or tackle a player from his unseen side (out of his vision).

BLISTERING SPEED
An exceptionally fast receiver, running back or kick-off/punt returner is said to have 'blistering' speed, and leaves trailing players sucking air.

BLITZ
An all-out attack by one or more defensive players on the quarterback, made before he can deliver the pass. If the attack is successful the quarterback is sacked for a big loss of yardage or even turns over the ball by a fumble. If however the quarterback can beat the blitz, especially with a pass, the defence gives up big yards, even a touchdown, as the blitzing players have vacated their normal position. Also called a dog or a red dog.

BLITZERS
The linebackers charging into the offensive backfield.

BLOCKING
The legal method of obstructing an opponent's progress by contacting him with any part of the blocker's body, but almost never below the waist. Also used to describe the method of hindering a team from scoring a field goal or a pat by blocking its flight to the goal-post, or from punting the ball downfield by throwing the body in front of the ball.

BLOCKING ASSIGNMENT
The task, for an offensive player, of obstructing the progress of a defensive player so as to allow the designated play to work.

BLOCKING BACK
The runningback in the backfield, whose primary responsibility on a specific play is to protect the ballcarrier or passer from on-rushing defenders.

BLOW AWAY
The action of the offensive line as it hammers the defensive line to open holes for the runningback or provide a good pass pocket for the quarterback.

BLOW DEAD
To signal the end of a play by blowing a whistle.

BLOWN COVERAGE
When the defensive back or linebacker does not shadow a potential receiver and the receiver then makes a catch for a long gain, the cover is blown.

BLUE CHIPPER
An exceptional high school or junior college player recruited to a major college and then engaged as a pro. Among pros, the players' opponents.

BOMB
A long, high, spiralling forward pass which looks like a bomb on its way to the target. This pass usually goes for long yardage or a touchdown.

BOMB SQUAD
A nickname for the punt/kick-off return team. Also called the suicide squad.

19

BOOKENDS
The two dominant offensive tackles or defensive ends whose leadership and aggressive play hold the rest of line together.

BOOTLEG
Against a strong pursuing team the quarterback will sometimes call a play which looks as though it will go a certain way. Instead, he keeps the ball hidden, tucked alongside his hip, and runs outside, sometimes with a lineman or receiver blocking in front. Also called a keep. If there are no blockers this is called a naked bootleg.

BOUNCING IT OUTSIDE
If the original play is intended to be run up the middle and the runningback finds that his path is completely blocked, he will keep the play alive by running to the outside of the line.

BOUNDARY LINES
Sidelines and endlines which define the length and width of a football field.

BOXMAN
One of the three members of the chain gang who is responsible for operating the downbox.

BREAD-AND-BUTTER PLAY
The favourite and most effective play on the offence. The team will rely on this play in a crucial situation.

BREADBASKET
The cupping action a receiver makes when he is about to catch the lofted ball.

BREAKAWAY BACK

A runner with good speed, strength and deception who can make a big play by getting by the defenders. Eric Dickerson of the LA Rams is such a player.

BREAKING A TACKLE

Escaping from the grip of a tackler (when carrying the ball) to gain extra yards.

BREAK OFF A BIG RUN

To make a big play which gains substantial yards.

BRICK WALL

A player or number of players who cannot be moved. Offensive units such as the Hogs (Washington Redskins (or the Monsters of the Midway (Chicago Bears) are typical examples.

BRING ON THE CHAINS
Chains, measuring exactly 10 yards in length, are used to mark the distance the team in possession has advanced the ball. The referee normally gives the sideline the order to carry the chains on.

BROKEN FIELD RUNNER
A player who has the ability to slip by defenders into the open field, darting, slashing and juking all the way to the end zone. Marcus Allen of the LA Raiders and Jim Brown of the 1950s/'60s Cleveland Browns are fine examples of such runners.

BROKEN PLAY
A planned offensive play which fails because of a mix-up between the quarterback and runningback or wide receiver. The quarterback will then be forced to improvise a play.

BRUSH BLOCK
One which allows the offensive player to impede the defensive player while he carries out another assignment. Also called a check.

BULA-BULA BACK
Used by some professional football scouts to describe a college runningback who is exceptional at carrying the ball but who is not especially good at catching the ball or blocking for others.

BULL

A big, powerful and quick runningback who bulldozes his way up the middle for tough yards. John Riggins (Washington Redskins) and Earl Campbell (New Orleans Saints) are formidable bulls. Also called a power back.

BULLET PASS

A hard, accurate pass which follows the trajectory of a rifle bullet. Also called a frozen rope, hummer or rifle shot.

BUMP AND RUN

Pass coverage by the defensive backs on receivers at the line of scrimmage. Once the ball is snapped the defensive back makes contact with the receiver in an effort to affect his timing and direction downfield.

BURNER

A wide receiver who has exceptional speed over a short area, which allows him to get away from defensive backs at the line of scrimmage and make the big catch.

BUTTONHOOK

A pass pattern in which the receiver runs downfield for about 15 yards, stops and suddenly makes a U-turn back towards the line of scrimmage and the quarterback. Also called a comeback pass, or just a hook.

BYE-BYE BLUES

Used by TV and radio commentators to describe a long run or big catch. After the ballcarrier has got by the defender he is said to give them the 'bye-bye blues'. Touchdown runs are also called 'goodnight, Irene', 'off to the races', 'open the door, Katie', 'school's out', 'that's all, she wrote', and 'turn out the lights'.

C

CADENCE
The quarterback's rhythmic call, which tells his teammates when the ball is about to be snapped.

CALL
A play selection.

CATCH-UP FOOTBALL
The kind of game most teams hate to play, having to come from behind to win. In the 1970s the Dallas Cowboys, with Roger 'the Dodger' Stabach at the helm, were great players of 'catch-up'.

CAUGHT IN A VICE
The situation of a defensive player who is blocked by *two* offensive players. See also double team.

CENTRE
The offensive lineman who starts the play by snapping the ball through his legs to the quarterback, punter or holder (for a field goal or extra point).

CEREBRAL PLAYER
Usually a player of great experience who makes up for his loss of speed and/or mobility with a good analytical brain. The ageing Jim Plunkett of the LA Raiders and Charlie Joiner of the San Diego Chargers are cerebral players.

CHAIN
The 10-yard device used to measure the distance a team has gained in order to keep possession of the ball after four downs.

CHAIN GANG
The assistants to the officials who stand on the sideline and operate the downbox (boxman) and the rods (rodmen). Also called the chain crew.

CHALK TALK
The team meeting in which strategy is discussed; plays are sometimes drawn on a blackboard with chalk.

CHECK
See brush block.

CHECK OFF
To call an audible or automatic.

CHICKEN FIGHT
A pass-blocking assignment by an offensive lineman in which he stands his opponent straight up.

CHIP SHOT
An easy field goal.

CHINESE BANDITS
The name coach Paul Dietzel gave to his ultra-aggressive defensive units when he coached at Louisiana State University and the Army Academy in the late 'fifties and early 'sixties.

CHUCK
To ward off a pass receiver coming across the line of scrimmage, to stop him getting downfield to execute a pass pattern.

CIRCUS CATCH
A near-impossible catch made by a receiver downfield. In the 1970s Lynon Swann and John Stallworth of the Pittsburgh Steelers made many brilliant circus catches.

CLEATS

The detachable or moulded plastic protrusions attached to the sole of the player's footwear which provide grip and traction during play.

CLIP

An illegal and highly dangerous form of blocking that consists of diving or throwing the body across the back of the legs of any other player than the ballcarrier. It is legal within 3 yards of the scrimmage, but outside that area is subject to a 15-yard penalty.

CLOCK PLAY

A defensive play specifically designed to stop the clock. This might be a sideline pass or pass attempt or a rushing play run out of bounds. *See* quarters.

CLOTHESLINE

A dangerous and illegal method of stopping a ballcarrier whereby an opponent thrusts his arm out sideways so that the ballcarrier's head or neck makes contact with the outstretched arm.

CLUTCH PLAY

The catching of an important pass (usually on a crucial third down play) by a receiver against all odds. Tony Hill and Drew Pearson of the Dallas Cowboys were two notable clutch players of recent years.

COFFIN CORNER

The strategic area inside the 10-yard line aimed for by the punters; a type of punt which goes out of bounds near the opponent's goal line.

COIN TOSS

The preliminary to the football game: the referee flips a coin in the presence of both team captains and the visiting captain makes the calls, 'heads' or 'tails'. The winning captain can opt to receive the opening kick-off, or select the goal to defend.

COLLEGE DRAFT
See draft.

COLOUR ANALYST/COMMENTATOR
Member of television/radio broadcast team responsible for explaining and interpreting the game action for viewers/listeners.

COMBINATION BLOCK
A manoeuvre in which the offensive, guard tackle or centre changes assignment to get a better angle on the defender.

COMEBACK PASS
See buttonhook.

COME OFF THE BALL
To fire aggressively off the line of scrimmage the moment the ball is snapped.

CONDITIONING
Football fitness training before and during the season.

CONTAINMENT
Holding off your opponent on the line – not really dominating him, just keeping him from making a big play.

CONVERSION
A one-point score immediately following a touchdown which is kicked through the goal post. In collegiate football a conversion can also be passed or run into the end zone: this is worth 2 points. Also called a point after touchdown, or PAT, or a try for point.

CO-OP BLOCKING
The action of two offensive linemen blocking one defensive lineman.

CORNERBACK
A defensive player who takes up a position about 5 or 10 yards from the line of scrimmage and a few yards from the side line. Lester Hayes and Mark Haynes (LA Raiders), Everson Walls (Dallas Cowboys) and Darron Cherry (Kansas City Chiefs) are some of today's best contemporary cornerbacks. Also called a halfback.

CORNERBACKER
Outside linebacker. Also called corner linebacker.

CORNER LINEBACKER
See cornerbacker.

COUGH UP THE BALL

A fumble which results in the loss of possession of the football.

COUNTER PLAY

A running play designed to catch the defence off guard by making all the initial movement one way while the play itself is going the other way.

COUNT SYSTEM

The method by which a quarterback and receiver work together by co-ordinating time and movement to complete a pass, e.g. first receiver in 3 seconds, second receiver in 4 seconds and so on.

CRACKBACK BLOCK

A dangerous and illegal blocking technique in which an offensive player, usually a pass receiver, blocks the defender from behind and below the waist within 5 yards of the line of scrimmage.

CRASH

To fire out quickly across the line of scrimmage into the offensive backfield: a defensive action.

CRAWLING

An illegal attempt to advance the ball after the player's body has touched the ground; this manoeuvre is particularly effective when several players in a pile-up block the officials' view. The penalty for this activity is the loss of 5 yards.

CRISS-CROSS

A passing pattern in which two receivers cross at a given spot downfield in an effort to confuse the defence. Also described as a crossing pattern.

CROSSBLOCK

An offensive line-blocking scheme in which assignments are exchanged. Also called a crossover.

CROSSING PATTERN
See criss-cross.

CROSSOVER
See crossblock.

CUP
A semi-circular pocket made up by offensive linemen to protect the passer from onrushing defensive linemen. Also called a pocket.

CURL
A pass pattern in which the receiver runs downfield, then turns inside and moves slightly back towards the quarterback.

CUT
A change in direction made by a ballcarrier.

CUTBACK
Doubling back against the flow of play: the ballcarrier runs to the outside, then changes direction and runs back inside.

CUT OFF BLOCK
To block a defender and thus allow running room for a ballcarrier.

CUTTING DOWN
Forcefully blocking or tackling an opponent to the ground.

D

D-BACK
Defensive back.

DAYLIGHT
A gap in the defensive line opened up by the offensive line to allow the runningback to go through.

DEAD BALL
The ball is dead when no longer in play.

DEAD RUN
A run at full speed.

DEEP MAN
The receiver furthest downfield as the quarterback is about to throw.

DEEP RECEIVER
See deep man.

DEFENCE
The team not in possession of the ball.

DEFENSIVE
Type of action taken by the team without the ball to keep the other team (with the ball) from scoring or advancing the ball downfield.

DEFENSIVE END
A defensive lineman positioned on the end of the line of scrimmage, outside the two defensive tackles.

DEFENSIVE HOLDING
An illegal act by a defender of holding or grabbing an offensive player; subject to a 10-yard penalty.

DEFENSIVE TACKLE
A defensive player positioned at the line of scrimmage between the two defensive ends.

DELAY
Action of a player momentarily holding his position at the line of scrimmage after the ball has been snapped, to fool the defenders into thinking he is not involved in the play. After the delay he then runs downfield to receive a pass or to block for a ballcarrier.

DELAY FLARE
A pass pattern in which a runningback either fakes or brushblocks a defender, then slips across the line of scrimmage to receive a pass. Also called a delay pass.

DELAY OF GAME

A team is allowed 25 seconds (college) or 30 seconds (professional) to put the ball into play. If the offence does not snap the ball in this time, the referee will impose a 5-yard penalty against them.

DELAY PASS

See delay flare.

DEPTH CHART

A reference chart which lists the starters and players held in reserve. The charts usually lists three players at all positions.

DIAGRAM

Coaches use diagrams so that each player knows his assignment on a particular play.

DIME

See dime back, dime defence.

DIME BACK
The sixth defensive back on passing down. Also called a dime. *See* dime defence.

DIME DEFENCE
A defensive alignment in which six backs are deployed.

DISQUALIFIED PLAYER
One who is ejected from the game, usually for a flagrant rule violation or unsportsmanlike conduct on the field.

DIVE
A straight-ahead running play in which the runningback takes the hand-off and plunges across the line of scrimmage for a short gain or touchdown.

DIVE BACK
The runningback set up directly behind the quarterback in the formation.

DIVE PLAY
See dive.

DOG
See blitz.

DOMINATION BLOCK
An overpowering block by an offensive lineman which takes the defender completely out of the play.

DON'T HIT HIM, HE'S DEAD
A phrase used by officials to stop the defenders from hitting the quarterback after he has released the pass.

DOUBLE FOUL
A rule violation by both teams during the same down.

DOUBLE MOTION
Starting to move one way then reversing and going the other way: a ploy used by receivers or runningbacks.

DOUBLE REVERSE
See reverse.

DOUBLE SLOT
An offensive formation in which one back sets up between tackle and tightend and another aligns between tackle and splitend.

DOUBLE TEAM
Two defensive players covering one pass receiver, or two offensive linemen blocking one defensive player, usually a lineman or linebacker. Also called a vice or a two-on-one.

DOUBLE WING
An offensive formation in which the quarterback sets up behind the centre, the fullback 4 yards behind the quarterback, with the flanker and halfback set on either end of the line of scrimmage.

DOWN

The action of an offensive team running with the ball or trying a pass. A team is allowed four downs in which to gain at least 10 yards. If it fails to make the necessary 10 yards during a particular four-down series, possession is transferred to the opposition.

DOWN AND IN

A pass pattern in which the receiver runs downfield for a given number of yards (usually 10 yards), fakes to the outside, then cuts sharply to the inside.

DOWN AND OUT

A pass pattern in which the receiver runs downfield for a given number of yards (usually 10 yards), fakes to the inside, then cuts sharply to the outside to the nearest sideline.

DOWNBOX

Official sideline equipment used to mark the spot of the ball for each play from scrimmage and indicate the down to be played. It consists of a rod at least 4 feet high on which numbered cards (1-4) are attached to designate the down in play.

DOWNFIELD

Once an offensive player has moved about 3 yards past the line of scrimmage, he is considered to be downfield. In passing situations offensive linemen are not allowed beyond the 3-yard area.

DOWNFIELD BLOCK

Any contact made with a defender 3 yards or more beyond the line of scrimmage.

DOWNING THE BALL

When a kick-off goes into the end zone, the kick-off returner can elect not to bring the ball out. If he goes down on one knee this gives his team the ball on their 20-yard line to begin play. Also called grounding the ball.

DRAFT

A system employed by the US National Football League to select the best collegiate players. It allows the team finishing with the worst won/lost record from the previous season to have the first pick. All the other teams select according to their won/lost records. The selection is made over 12 rounds and is the biggest day in the pro football year.

DRAW

An offensive running play in which the quarterback drops back as if to pass but instead hands off to a runningback who runs right by the hard-charging defenders.

DRIVE

The ballcarrier's ability to gain yardage despite heavy contact by defenders; also the movement downfield by an offensive team during a successful series of downs.

DRIVE BLOCK
To block a defender by using the shoulder as the main point of contact to clear a path for the ballcarrier; a ploy used by offensive players.

DROP BACK
What the quarterback does as he retreats from the line of scrimmage, getting ready to pass the ball or initiate a draw play. Also called fade back.

DROP KICK
To boot the football as it touches the ground.

DUCKBALL
An ugly, wobbly pass which looks like a wounded duck in flight. Also called a flutterball or a knuckle ball.

DUMP OFF
To throw to an uncovered receiver, usually a runningback deployed primarily as a blocker. The San Francisco 49ers' quarterback Joe Montana and runningback Roger Craig have made this type of pass an art form.

E

EAT THE BALL
If a quarterback accepts a tackle for a loss of yards rather than risk throwing a pass which could be intercepted, he is eating the ball.

ELIGIBLE RECEIVER

Only five offensive players are permitted ('eligible') to catch, or receive, a forward pass: the two ends, the halfback, the fullback and the flanker back.

ENCROACHMENT

Stepping to the neutral zone prior to snapping the ball – an action subject to a 5-yard penalty.

END (DEFENSIVE)

The two players at each end of the line of scrimmage, on the defensive team.

END (OFFENSIVE)

The two players at each end of the line of scrimmage, on the offensive team.

END AROUND

An offensive play in which the tightend or wide receiver going in one direction takes the ball from a runningback (or quarterback) going in the other direction. *See* reverse.

END LINE

The boundary marking at the back of the end zone.

END SWEEP

A running play around the left or right end of the line of scrimmage. Marcus Allen of the LA Raiders is a great exponent of this play. Also known as a sweep. *See also* student body right.

END ZONE

The touchdown area, 10 yards deep and 53 yards 1 foot wide.

EXECUTION
To carry out a pre-designed play.

EXPANSION TEAM
Every so often the US National Football League grants a franchise to some lucky millionaire and his consortium. For the first few years while the team establishes itself it is called an expansion team.

EXTRA POINT
The point after touchdown. *See* conversion.

F

FACE GUARDING
An illegal arm or hand movement by the pass defender that obstructs the receiver's vision.

FACE MASK
See birdcage.

FADE BACK
See drop back.

FAIR CATCH
When a punt returner sees the coverage team coming up fast, he can decide not to return the ball; he then calls for a 'fair catch', which he takes by reaching his hands above his head; while doing this he may not be touched by a defender.

FAKE
An action by the quarterback in which he simulates handing off the ball to a runningback and then passes to a receiver, or simulates a pass then hands off to a runningback.

FAST START
The action of the runningback getting to the line of scrimmage quickly as soon as the ball is snapped.

FEARSOME FOURSOME

The famed LA Rams' defensive front four during the late 'sixties and 'seventies, which included All-Pros Merlin Olsen and Deacon Jones, Lamar Lundy and Roosevelt Grier.

FEATHER THE BALL

As well as being able to throw bullet passes downfield a quarterback must be able to finesse the ball to a receiver. The 49ers' Joe Montana is a master of this type of pass.

FIELD GENERAL

The quarterback.

FIELD GOAL

This is achieved by kicking the ball through the uprights and over the crossbars after the ball has been snapped to a holder kneeling 7 yards behind the line of scrimmage.

FIELD GOAL RANGE

The area from which a team's field goalkicker can realistically kick a field goal.

FIELD JUDGE

The game official whose primary duties include timing the intermission between periods and each half, the length of each time out and the 25- or 30-second clock. He also covers the downfield action on passes, kicks or punts.

FIELD OF PLAY

The area on which the game is played. It is 120 yards long x 53$\frac{1}{3}$ yards wide bounded by sidelines and goal lines.

FIELD POSITION
The position on the field occupied by the team in possession of the ball, which will determine the type of plays called by the coach.

FILLING THE GAP
Occupying the space vacated by a teammate who has moved out to lead the interference on a running play; used of offensive linemen.

FIND THE SEAM
To find the softest area in the defence. When a quarterback finds a receiver in the seam he will more often than not get a completion.

FIRE OUT
To explode off the line of scrimmage as soon as the ball is snapped.

FIRST DOWN
The initial play in a series of four downs.

FIRST STRING
The players who begin the game.

FIRST STRINGER
The starting player at a position.

FIRST TEAM
The best players on offence and defence.

FLAG

At the four corners of the goal line at each end of the field stand small pylons, called flags, planted in the ground. Their name dates back to the time when spring-loaded flags were used in the end zone. Also a pass pattern in which the receiver runs downfield and cuts diagonally to the outside, towards the end zone pylons. *See also* penalty marker.

FLAG FOOTBALL

An inexpensive and cheap version of football where no tackling is allowed and every player is eligible to score. Each player wears a flag-like streamer attached to his belt, and which must be removed if a runner or receiver is to be stopped.

FLAG ON THE PLAY

See penalty marker.

FLAK JACKET

A special lightweight vest with padding to protect the ribs, usually worn by quarterbacks with rib injuries.

FLANK

The area between the flankerback and the sideline. *See also* flat.

FLANKER

An offensive receiver positioned at least 2 yards behind

the line of scrimmage and up to 6 yards outside the tightend.

FLANKERBACK
An offensive backfield player.

FLARE-OUT
A runningback circling out of the backfield to catch a pass.

FLARE PASS
A short pass thrown to a runningback behind the line of scrimmage. Also called a flat pass.

FLAT
The area of the playing field behind and outside the line of scrimmage.

FLAT BALL
A ball position for an onside kick attempt.

FLAT PASS
See flare pass.

FLEA-FLICKER
A razzle-dazzle play which is a spectacular crowd-pleaser when it works but looks pretty bad when it

doesn't. The quarterback hands off to a back who runs up to the line of scrimmage, turns and pitches the ball back to the quarterback, by which time the linebackers and the defensive back should have swallowed the bait on the run fake, leaving a receiver wide open for a catch – which will be a long gainer or a touchdown. Also known as gimmick play.

FLEX DEFENCE
A run-orientated defensive alignment invented and used almost exclusively by the Dallas Cowboys.

FLIP
A short, quick pass.

FLIP-FLOP
A defensive manoeuvre in which players switch sides of field.

FLOOD
To send two or more pass receivers covered by defenders into the same area of the defensive zone in order to confuse the defensive backs and increase the quarterback's chances of completing the pass.

FLOOD FORMATION

An offensive formation in which three or more receivers line up to the outside of one side of the field. *See also* satellite express.

FLUTTERBALL

A wobbly, ungainly pass which goes end over end downfield. Also called a duckball.

FLYING WEDGE

A formation used pre-1914 in which ten players formed a V-shaped wedge, linking arms to fend off tacklers. Happily this formation has now been banned as it caused many injuries.

FLY PATTERN

A pass pattern in which a receiver runs straight downfield as fast as he can, hoping to beat the defender with sheer speed. To fly means the same as to go. Also called square out and down.

FOOTSTEPS

When a receiver is about to make a tough catch (especially in the middle of the field) he sometimes anticipates, through some sixth sense, a hit from unseen defenders which could cause him to drop the ball. This is called 'hearing footsteps'.

FORCE

When a cornerback or safety turns or contains a running play to the inside and helps to make the tackle he is said to be 'making the force'.

FORCING THE BALL
See throw into a crowd/traffic.

FORTY
The classic distance in football: 40 yards. The running drill, consisting of a series of timed sprints over this distance, determines players' speed and acceleration.

FORWARD FUMBLE
A play, now outlawed, in which a ballcarrier deliberately fumbles the ball, hoping it will be recovered by a teammate or go out of bounds far enough ahead to gain additional yards.

FORWARD LATERAL
The quarterback passes the ball forward of the line of scrimmage to a receiver who then laterals the ball to a trailing teammate, who runs it into the end zone. Also called a hitch-and-trailer.

FORWARD MOTION
The furthest point of a ballcarrier's progress downfield. Also called forward progress.

FORWARD PASS
Throwing the ball toward the opponent's goal line to an eligible receiver.

FORWARD PROGRESS
See forward motion.

FORWARD WALL
The interior offensive line: left and right tackles, left and right guard and centre.

FOUL
Any violation of a playing rule. *See* penalty, rule infraction.

FOUR HORSEMEN OF NOTRE-DAME
Four well-known backfield players from the University of Notre-Dame (the Fighting Irish) in the early 'twenties. They were Elmer Layden (fullback), Don Miller (halfback), Jim Crowley (halfback) and Harry Stuhdreher (quarterback).

FOUR-THREE DEFENCE
An alignment characterized by four down linemen at the line of scrimmage and three linebackers.

FRANCHISE PLAYER
An exceptional player who can transform the fortunes of a team. O.J. Simpson of the Buffalo Bills is a good example from the 1970s, Dan Marino (Miami Dolphins), Walter Payton (Chicago Bears) and Curt Warner (Seattle Seahawks) are contemporary examples. Also called a monied-back.

FREE AGENT
A player whose services are no longer required and is free to sell his services to another team; alternatively, a player not drafted by any team who goes to training camp hoping to make the team.

FREE BALL
A live ball not in the possession of either team. If the ball becomes free because of a fumble or muffed punt/kick-off reception, the first player to get hold of the ball will gain possession for his team.

FREE KICK

The action of putting the ball into play after a safety, field goal or point after touchdown, and the start of each half of the game. The receiving team is not allowed to interfere with the kicker.

FREE-KICK DOWN

A play which begins with a free kick.

FREE SAFETY

A defensive back who is not specifically responsible for any receiver but freewheels in the defensive backfield, ready to assist any other defender with his coverage.

FREQUENCY CHART

A detailed breakdown of an opponent's offensive and defensive tendencies.

FREQUENCY READING

A study of an opponent's plays and play reactions, made in order to work out possible counter-manoeuvres.

FRESHMAN

A first-year high school or college player.

FRONT FOUR

A defensive line consisting of two defensive ends and two defensive tackles.

FROZEN ROPE

A quick, hard, bullet-type pass aimed at the receiver's chest. *See also* bullet pass, on the money, on the numbers, throw the rock.

FULLBACK
One of the four offensive backfield players, he is usually a strong, heavy player mostly called upon to carry the ball up the middle for short yardage or block for a smaller, quicker ballcarrier or the quarterback in certain passing downs.

FULL HOUSE BACKFIELD
See basic T.

FUMBLE
A dropped or mishandled ball, resulting usually from the player in possession being tackled or letting the ball slip from his hands.

FUMBLE ROOSKI
A razzle-dazzle trick play popularized by the Nebraska (University) Cornhuskers, in which the quarterback deliberately fumbles the snap from centre. He then pulls to the right as if handing-off to a back; the left guard and right tackle pull out as if to block for the back; however, the right guard picks up the ball and runs to the left, aiming for big yardage. Offensive guard Dean Steinkuhler used this play to score a spectacular touchdown during the 1983 Orange Bowl against the University of Miami.

FUNDAMENTALIST
A conservative coach who believes strongly in the basics of football, like running the ball, basic blocking or tackling and a short- to medium-range passing game.

FUNDAMENTALS
The basic skills of players, including, on offence, block-

ing, running, passing and catching, and, on defence, tackling, defending against the run and passing.

G

GAME BALL
A ball awarded to a player for a special reason, e.g. breaking a record or scoring his first touchdown.

GAME PLAN
The detailed game strategy produced before a game to highlight what the team will do in a given situation on offence, defence or special team.

GAMER
A player who will play despite pain, injury or illness and who has an overwhelming desire to win. Also used to describe a player who hates or is an indifferent performer at practice but saves himself for the game.

GANG TACKLE
Several defenders contriving to stop a ballcarrier. Also called a multiple tackle.

GAP
The distance or spacing between two offensive or two defensive linemen. Gaps are numbered by coaches to indicate the direction of an offensive or defensive play.

GET AN ANGLE
To gain a blocking advantage on a defender.

GET OFF THE BALL
To fire off the offensive line once the ball has been snapped.

GIMME
When a ball is passed with great accuracy to a receiver, this is called a 'gimme'. (TV commentators may be heard to say, 'He dropped the gimme.')

GIMMICK PLAY
See flea-flicker.

GIRDLE PADS
Plastic-covered foam rubber protective attire for lower back and hips.

GO
See fly pattern.

GO AGAINST THE GRAIN
To move against the flow and direction of play.

GOAL
The area between the two uprights and the crossbars between which the ball must travel in order to score on a field goal or PAT (point after touchdown).

GOAL LINE
The thick chalk line which designates the beginning of the scoring area, the end zone. It is only necessary for the ball to be over the line for a player to score a touchdown.

GOAL LINE DEFENCE
A defensive alignment which calls for six or seven big linemen to stop a short-yardage running play.

GOAL LINE STAND
An all-out attempt by the defence to keep the offensive team from scoring a touchdown.

GOAL POSTS
Two vertical posts in each end zone set 18 feet 6 inches apart and connected by a crossbar 10 feet above the ground. In collegiate and high school football, the vertical posts are set 23 feet 4 inches apart. Also called uprights.

GOAL TO GO
The series of plays run from inside the 10-yard line from which no other first downs can be attained without a touchdown.

GO FOR IT
To attempt a high-risk play. Sometimes on the fourth down, for example, a coach may decide not to punt or go for a field goal but try to make the first down or touchdown instead.

GO NORTH AND SOUTH
To run straight ahead without getting fancy: simply an attempt to move the ball forward.

GOODNIGHT, IRENE
A long touchdown pass or run.

GRANDSTAND QUARTERBACK
See armchair quarterback.

GRASP AND CONTROL RULE
A judgement call by the referee in which the ball is whistled dead the moment the quarterback attempting to pass is in the hands of a defender and cannot free himself; the rule was designed to prevent quarterback injury.

GREEN GRIPPER TOWEL
The small towel worn by wide receivers and defensive backs which used to be covered in 'stickum' (an adhesive substance) to aid ball-catching. The use of any adhesive substance to aid catching has now been outlawed.

GRIDDER
Any football player.

GRIDIRON
The football playing field.

GRINDING IT OUT
Advancing the ball downfield through a series of short running and passing plays.

GROUNDING THE BALL
Throwing an incomplete forward pass to an area in which there is no eligible receiver, in order to avoid being tackled for loss of yardage. A judgement call by an official which results in a loss of down and a 15-yard penalty. Also called intentional grounding.

GUARDS
The offensive linemen on the line of scrimmage set up next to the centre.

GUN-SHY

A player who is very cautious and tries to avoid contact wherever possible, possibly because of an injury or hard hit in a previous game or on a previous play.

GUT

The toughest way to gain yardage. The quarterback rams the ball into the stomach of the runningback, who then tries to run up the middle – usually right between the centre and the guard. One of the best exponents of this ploy was John Riggins, formerly of the Washington Redskins.

H

HAIL MARY

A desperation pass, usually thrown deep downfield in the dying seconds of the game. The quarterback throws the ball to an area flooded by players from both sides and prays that the ball will be caught by one of his players in or near the end zone.

HALF

The midpoint of a game; two quarters or periods (first and second or third and fourth) of the playing time.

HALFBACK (DEFENSIVE)
See cornerback.

HALFBACK (OFFENSIVE)
One of four offensive backfield players: the lighter, faster of the two runningbacks in a two-back formation. He is the primary ballcarrier on most running plays.

HALFBACK OPTION
Any offensive play in which a halfback can choose to continue to run or throw a forward pass.

HALF-TIME
A 20-minute interval between the second and third quarters.

HAND FIGHTER
A defensive lineman who uses his hands to ward off an offensive blocker.

HAND OFF
To place the ball in the hands of a ballcarrier; used of quarterbacks.

HANG TIME

The number of seconds a punt stays in the air. The longer the hang time, the better the chance of the punt team preventing a return.

HASH MARKS

The inbound lines between the 5-yard line markers, spaced one yard apart, which are used to fix the point where the ball will be put in play.

H-BACK

An offensive player deployed as a second tightend in single back formation.

HEADHUNTER

A tough, defensive player who is always trying to making a lasting impression on his opponent by hitting him hard, legally or otherwise.

HEAD LINESMAN

An official positioned at the line of scrimmage who is primarily responsible for offside calls, chain crew, marking forward progress, spotting ineligible receivers downfield and marking where the spot ball goes out of bounds on his side of the field.

HEAD SLAP

Illegally hitting or striking an opponent on the side of the head; subject to a 15-yard penalty.

HEARING FOOTSTEPS

See footsteps.

HEAVY HITTER

An aggressive blocker or tackler.

HEISMAN TROPHY

The award given annually to the top college football player in the US, as determined by the votes of sportswriters and broadcasters throughout the nation.

HELLO-GOODBYE SPEED

First used to describe the velocity of the two exceptionally quick Miami Dolphins receivers, Mark Clayton and Mark Duper.

HELMET

Protective headgear worn by football players: a plastic shell padded with air-filled sponge-rubber tubes, or air and glycol segments.

HIDEOUT PLAY

An illegal call in which an offensive player lingers near

the sideline during his team's huddle, hoping to gain advantage by not being seen when the ball is snapped.

HI-DIDDLE-DIDDLE

A spectacular short-yardage play in which a runningback leaps over the pile of bodies to gain the touchdown or first down. Marcus Allen (Los Angeles Raiders), Hershel Walker (Dallas Cowboys) and Walter Payton (Chicago Bears) are some of the best exponents of this play. Also called hurdling and over the top.

HIGH FIVE

A post-touchdown celebration in which two players run towards each other, leap in the air and slap hands above their heads. It was popularized by James Lofton and John Jefferson of the Green Bay Packers.

HIGH-LOW

Blocking by two offensive players, one making contact with the upper part of a defender's body while his teammate tackles low; also, similar mode of tackling by two defensive players.

HIGH STEPPING

Running, while carrying the ball, with an exaggerated high-knee action. San Francisco 49ers runningback Roger Craig, who was a hurdler at the University of Nebraska, is a great high-stepper.

HIGHTOPS

The old-fashioned black over-the-ankle leather shoes once worn by football players. These have now been replaced by the more popular low-cut white shoes.

HIKE
See snapping the ball.

HITCH-AND-GO
See hook and go.

HITCH-AND-TRAILER
See forward lateral.

HITCH PASS
A quick spring downfield by a receiver followed by a quick turn back toward the quarterback to catch a pass.

HIT-THE-HOLE
To run at full speed to a point of attack at the line of scrimmage; used of runningbacks.

HOLD AND RELEASE
See delay.

HOLDING
Using the hands illegally to impede an opponent.

HOME RUN
A long touchdown pass.

HOOK
See buttonhook.

HOOK-AND-GO
A pass pattern in which receiver runs downfield, stops, comes back one or two steps toward the passer, then turns downfield again. Also called a hitch-and-go or a turn-and-go.

HORSE
A powerful runningback who is very hard to stop and can be relied on to gain extra yards. Also called a power back.

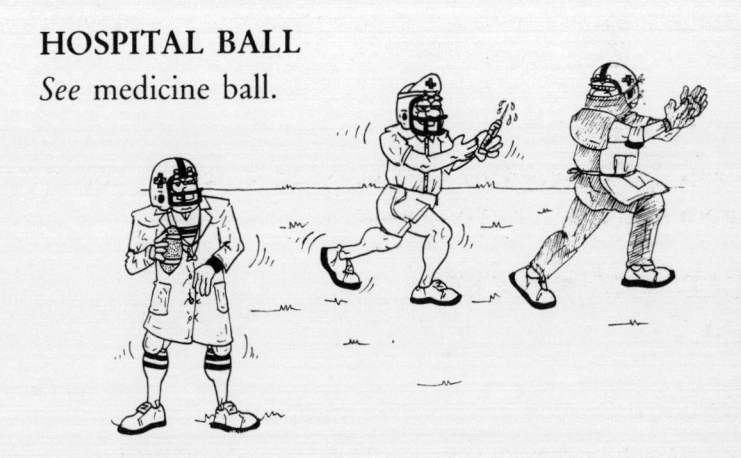

HOSPITAL BALL
See medicine ball.

HOT DOG
A player who is prone to excessive celebration after a big play (touchdown, interceptions, sack, fumble recovery, etc.). Well-known examples include the Atlanta Falcons' 'White Shoes' Johnson (the splits); the Denver Broncos' Butch Johnson (the earthquake shuffle); the New York Jets' Mark Gastineau (the sack dance) and the Chicago Bears' Jim McMahon (the head butt). In 1984 the pro league barred any premeditated and excessive celebration, for which it became jokingly known as the No Fun League (NFL).

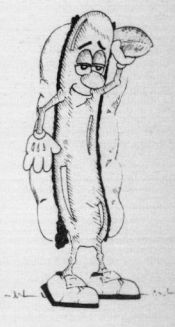

HOT HAND
A quarterback who is having a successful game or season passing the ball – as reflected in the high percentage rate of his pass completions.

HUDDLE
The gathering-together of players on offence and defence to discuss the plan for the next play.

HUMMER
See bullet pass or frozen rope.

HURDLING
See hi-diddle-diddle.

HURRY-UP OFFENCE
A game plan designed to squeeze the maximum amount of offensive plays out of the minimum amount of time, normally without a huddle, in the last two minutes of a half or of the game. The ploy also stops the defence from making any chances. Also called a two-minute drill.

I

I-BACK
Runningbacks in an I-formation.

I-FORMATION
An offensive formation in which three backfield players (quarterback and two runningbacks) set up in a single line behind the centre to form an I.

ILLEGAL FORWARD PASS
A ball thrown from beyond the line of scrimmage.

ILLEGAL MOTION
See in motion.

ILLEGAL PROCEDURE
A penalty called against a movement on the line of scrimmage just prior to the snap, or for having too few players on field. Also, an illegal alignment prior to the snap.

IMMACULATE RECEPTION
In the 1972 American football conference divisional play-off between the Pittsburgh Steelers and the Oakland Raiders, the Steelers were trailing 7-6 with 22 seconds left in the game and facing a crucial fourth and 10 situation on their own 40-yard line. Quarterback Terry Bradshaw dropped back to pass to runningback Frenchy Fuqua. Just as he was about to make the catch, Raider cornerback Jack ('The Assassin') Tatum managed to knock away the ball, which landed in the hands of Steelers runningback Franco Harris, who streaked down

the field untouched into the end zone to give the Steelers a come-from-behind victory, hence the 'immaculate reception'.

IMPACT PLAYER
A player who because of his outstanding ability can change the course of the game.

IMPETUS
Player action which gives momentum to the ball; also, a technical ruling on ball flight to determine possession in the event of a fumble.

IN
A pass pattern in which a receiver runs straight downfield then cuts sharply to the middle of the field. Also called an in-break.

INBOUND LINES
The hashmarks which are drawn parallel to the sidelines where the ball is put into play after going out of bounds. In professional football the hashmarks are 70 feet from the sidelines; in collegiate and high-school football they are 53 feet from the sidelines.

INBOUND MARKERS
See inbound lines.

INBOUNDS
The field of play.

IN-BREAK
See in.

INCOMPLETE PASS
A forward pass which is not caught.

INELIGIBLE RECEIVER
When a team is in possession, only five men are allowed downfield to catch a pass. They are the runningbacks, splitend, tightend and flanker. Anyone else on that team who catches the ball is called an ineligible receiver and is subject to a penalty.

IN-FLIGHT BALL
A ball still in the air after a forward pass, punt, kick, fumble or lateral.

INFLUENCE
Offensive line assignment in which a dominant lineman will pull to the outside to lure defenders away from the play.

INJURED RESERVE
At present in professional football each team is limited to 45 players only; if a player is hurt he is placed on reserve so as to allow the team to find a replacement to make up the 45-man roster.

IN MOTION
Running parallel to the line of scrimmage before the ball is snapped. This can only be done by one backfield player; all other players must remain in a set position.

INSIDE
The area along the line of scrimmage between offensive tackles. Also known as the interior line.

INSIDE CORNER
One of four points on the playing field where the goal line intersects the sideline.

INSIDE HAND-OFF
Offensive manoeuvre in which the exchange between quarterback and runner takes place behind the interior linemen.

INSIDE SLIP
See slant pass.

INSTANT REPLAY
An NFL official who sits in the press box may review the outcome of a certain play, e.g. a fumble, touchdown, player stepping out of bounds, or a dispute, by viewing it in slow motion on an instant-replay video provided by one of the TV networks covering the game (as many as 28 cameras cover NFL games, from all angles).

INTENTIONAL GROUNDING
A penalty awarded to a passer who deliberately throws the ball away in order to save being sacked for a loss of yards. *See also* grounding the ball.

INTERCEPTION
A forward pass caught by a defensive player instead of by the offensive pass receiver.

INTERFERENCE
Illegally hindering an opposing player who is attempting to catch a forward pass.

INTERIOR LINE
See inside.

INTERIOR LINEMEN
Offensive centre, guards and tackles.

IN THE GRASP
A ruling made to protect professional quarterbacks from unnecessary injury. If the defender breaks through the line of scrimmage and grabs the quarterback who then gets away it is recorded as a sack.

IN THE TRENCHES
Where the action is at the moment the ball is snapped. The hand-to-hand battles between offensive and defensive linemen have been compared to the trench warfare of World War I.

INTO TRAFFIC
Into an area which is covered by most defenders.

IRREGULAR
Used of special blocking assignments on running and passing plays.

ISOLATION BLOCK
Contact by an offensive back on a defensive lineman at or near the point of attack.

ISOLATION PLAY
An offensive manoeuvre designed to pull a defensive lineman out of position so that a player can run through the gap he leaves.

IT'S HISTORY
Commentator's phrase for the winning touchdown.

J

JAM
To stop a receiver legally as he tries to come off the line of scrimmage and run his pass pattern.

JERSEY
Part of a player's uniform, worn over the shoulder pads, in team colours and displaying the player's number, his name or the name of his team.

JERSEY NUMBERS
The official system which identifies players by the numbers on their uniforms.

JOG STEP
A short, choppy, stepping movement.

JUKE
A faking move by the ballcarrier used to elude a potential tackler; a manoeuvre made by the pass receiver to avoid a defender's close coverage.

JUKE STEP
Fancy running by a ballcarrier, dancing from side to side. Also called a stutter step.

JUKING
See stunting.

JUMP PASS
An offensive play manoeuvre in which the quarterback

leaps up to throw a ball over charging, arm-waving defenders.

JUNIOR
A third-year high-school or college player.

K

KAMIKAZE CORPS
See special teams.

KARDIAC KIDS
The name for a team which is well known for its close finishes. In the 1970s the New England Patriots and the Cleveland Browns were two such teams.

KEEP
To maintain possession of the ball; e.g. 'The quarterback keeps'.

KEEPER
See bootleg.

KEEP THE DRIVE ALIVE
To do everything to keep the plays moving downfield; used of the offence.

KEY

To shadow a player; if there is an exceptional player (or players) on offence (for instance, a very fast receiver or a breakaway back), he will be shadowed wherever he goes by several defenders to stop him from making the big play.

KEY

See tip-off.

KEY BLOCK

The vital block by an offensive player to spring a teammate.

KICKER

A special teams player who punts or place kicks the ball.

KICKING GAME

A team's ability to punt, kick field goals and kick-off.

KICKING TEE

A rubber or plastic contour mould in which the ball is set to facilitate kick-off; in collegiate and high-school football it is used to kick a field goal or PAT.

KICKING UNIT

A special team deployed for punts, field goal attempts, PATs and kick-offs. *See* suicide squad.

KICK-OFF

A free kick used to put the ball in play at the start of the game and of the second half, or after a PAT attempt or a successful field goal.

KICK-OUT BLOCK

Contact with a defender that forces him to the outside and allows the ballcarrier to cut inside.

KILL THE CLOCK

To exploit plays – usually running plays – designed to use as much time as possible. *See also* run out the clock.

KLEENEX PLAY

A razzle-dazzle trick play which is used once and then discarded, like the paper tissue.

KNEE PADS

Foam contour padding worn over the knee which allows the player maximum protection without impeding mobility.

KNOCKING AT THE DOOR
Pushing at the opposition's goal line, having advanced all the way down the field.

KNUCKLE BALL
See duck ball.

L

LATE HIT
The act of making contact after the ball is dead; subject to a 15-yard penalty.

LATERAL
Backward or sideways pass from one player to another.

LAYING-IN-THE-BUSHES
Waiting for a ballcarrier to come your way; used of defenders.

LAY THE LEATHER
To hit another player very hard (a term dating back to the days when players wore leather helmets).

LEAD
To throw a pass accurately ahead of a receiver so that he may catch it without breaking his stride. To pull out from a guard or tackle position to block a secondary or act as an optional blocker.

LEADING GUARD
See on guard.

LEADING TACKLE
See on tackle.

LEG WHIP
An outlawed practice in which one player on the ground kicks his legs wildly to try to stop an opponent; subject to a 10-yard penalty.

LINEBACKER

A defensive player who lines up behind the defensive linemen and in front of the defensive backs. He is usually the best athlete on the team because the position requires good speed, strength, agility and perception. Also called a plugger.

LINEBACKER CONTROL

The maximum split of a tightend that will enable him to keep the linebacker in a head-to-head position.

LINE DRIVE

Normally a punter or a kicker hangs the ball high, making it fairly easy to catch, but on a line drive he kicks it hard and flat, hoping it will bounce around and be difficult to catch.

LINE JUDGE

An official whose responsibilities include timing the game, recording time outs and the score, watching for illegal motion or shifts and marking out of bounds on his side of field.

LINEMEN

Offensive and defensive players on the line of scrimmage: centres, guards, tackles and ends.

LINE OF SCRIMMAGE

The imaginary line running from sideline to sideline where the ball is placed before the start of each play. The offence lines up with the ball and the defence lines up on the other side with a neutral zone in between.

LINESMAN

The official responsible for all the actions that take place at the line of scrimmage (such as offside). The head linesman tries to follow all the action on his side of the field and is also in charge of the chain crew.

LINE SURGE
The forward movement of the offensive and defensive lines that takes place the moment the ball is snapped.

LIVE BALL
Football in play.

LIVE COLOUR
Pre-designated colour code which alters the offensive team to an automatic; the colour code of an audible call made by the quarterback that precedes the automatic. This signals the offensive team to discount the play called in huddle.

LOAF OF BREAD
A precarious and ill-advised way of carrying a football, holding it in the hand like carrying a loaf of bread from the shop. It can often lead to a fumble.

LOFTED PASS
A long, high pass. *See also* alley-oops.

LOMBARDI TROPHY
The award, named after the legendary Green Bay Packers' coach, Vince Lombardi, made every year to the top defensive college player.

LONG GAINER
An offensive play which results in a substantial gain of yardage.

LONG MAN
The pass receiver moving furthest downfield.

LONG SIDE
That side of an unbalanced line which has most linemen.

LOOK-IN PASS
A play in which the quarterback straightens up immediately after taking the snap from centre instead of dropping back and throwing to a tightend or flanker moving diagonally toward the inside. Also called a look pass.

LOOK OFF
In order to give his receiver more time to get into the open, a good quarterback will always look away from the intended receiver to deceive the defenders.

LOOK PASS
See look-in pass.

LOOPING
Defensive linemen or linebackers sometimes exchange assignments and instead of charging straight ahead will loop around to an area vacated by another teammate.

LOOSE BALL
A ball not in a player's possession but in play. Usually the result of a fumble or muffed kick or punt return.

LOSS OF DOWN
An additional penalty assessment calling for forfeiture of play in a given series; part of the penalty for such violations as intentionally grounding a forward pass.

LOST THE HANDLE
Fumbled the snap.

LOWCUTS
Oxford-style football shoes worn by players today.

M

MAKE THE CUT
A player who has made it through a team's mandatory reduction at training camp.

MACK TRUCK
A very tough and strong defensive player.

MAN-FOR-MAN
Pass coverage by the defensive secondary where every potential pass receiver is shadowed by either a cornerback, a safety or even linebackers.

MAN-HEAD-ON
The opposing lineman on the line of scrimmage.

MAN-IN-MOTION
The offensive player moving in a lateral or backward direction from the line of scrimmage prior to the snap. *See also* in motion.

MAN OVER
A defensive deployment in which a lineman is set to one side of the offensive lineman.

MANSTER
A very tough defensive player, usually a lineman or

linebacker, who is considered by opponents to be half man and half monster.

MASSAGE HIS BACK
To hit the passer in the back from the blindside.

MEASURING CHAIN
See chain.

MEAT GRINDER
The area of an opposing team's greatest resistance. The offensive line of the Washington Redskins, the linebacking crew of the New York Giants and the defensive backfield of the Los Angeles Raiders have all been known to 'grind up' an opponent or two.

MEDICINE BALL
A very dangerous pass over the middle in heavy traffic. In the old days defenders used to say, 'Let him catch the ball and go to hospital for his medicine'. Also called a hospital ball.

MESSENGER
A player responsible for bringing in the play called from the sidelines. When Paul Brown was coaching the Cleveland Browns in the mid-'fifties he had a messenger guard system which employed two offensive linemen of approximately equal ability who would substitute for each other on alternate plays, rushing to the huddle to tell the quarterback what play coach Brown wanted called.

MIDDLE
The centre of the offensive line, usually the area between tackles.

MIDDLE GUARD
A defensive player lined across from offensive centre in 3-4 alignment.

MIDDLE LINE BACKER
A defensive player usually positioned 3-4 yards behind the line of scrimmage and between defensive tackles; often called defensive quarterback in 4-3 deployment.

MIDFIELD
The 50-yard line.

MISDIRECTION
See counter.

MISSISSIPPI GAMBLER
A coach with a reputation for taking risks. Also called a riverboat gambler.

MOMENTUM
A general feeling that things are going your way. A most important, though intangible, element of a football game which can be sensed whether you are on the field or in the stands. When a team has everything going its way it gathers momentum on both offence and defence, like an avalanche rushing down a mountainside.

MONDAY-MORNING QUARTERBACK
See armchair quarterback.

MONIED-BACK

A very well-paid runningback.
See franchise player.

MONSTER BACK

A defensive player who has no set position but lines himself up on the spot where he expects the play to develop and where he feels he is needed.

MONSTERS OF THE MIDWAY

The current Chicago Bears defence.

MOVE THE PILE

To push back the defensive line; used of the offensive line, it usually means the team is having a good day running the football.

MULTIPLE FOUL

Two or more rule infractions by one team during the same down.

MULTIPLE OFFENCE

See multiple set.

MULTIPLE SET

An offence that never looks the same way twice. It can have two backs running out of the 'I'; it can have the quarterback alone behind the centre with all the other backs moving out as pass receivers; it can have the tightend moving into the backfield. At times, it can combine all those elements and more. Also called a multiple offence.

N

NAIA
The National Association of Intercollegiate Athletics.

NAIL
To stop a ballcarrier or passer with a hard hit.

NAKED REVERSE

An offensive running play in which one back takes a hand-off from the quarterback and then heads in a certain direction, handing-off to another player heading in the opposite direction, who then runs up the field without any blockers.

NCAA

The National Collegiate Athletic Association, the rules of which organization provide the basis for all forms of American football.

NEAR BACK

The offensive backfield player nearest to the side where the play will be run.

NECESSARY LINE

The line to which the team in possession must advance the ball in order to maintain possession.

NEUTRAL ZONE

The area between the offensive and defensive lines of scrimmage, which is about as wide as the length of a football; also, the 10-yard area between free-kick lines of deployment.

NFC
The National Football Conference, a competitive unit of the NFL.

NFL
The National Football League, the major professional football organization in the USA.

NFLPA
The National Football League Players' Association: a players' union within the NFL.

NICKEL BACK
The fifth defensive back who replaces a linebacker in obvious passing situations.

NICKEL DEFENCE
A defensive alignment in which five defensive backs are deployed. A prevent defence designed for obvious passing situations.

NORTH-SOUTH RUNNER
An unspectacular runner who runs straight ahead downfield without any fancy moves. He is usually a big, bruising fullback such as ex-Washington Redskins runningback John Riggins, or the Cincinnati Bengals' Larry Kinnerbrew.

NOSE GUARD
A defensive lineman in the middle of a 5-2 or 3-4 defensive alignment.

NO SHOWS
The spectators who purchase tickets for a game but do not show up. This is an important statistic in televised pro football in the US as it will help determine whether or not a game is blacked out in the local area (*see* blackout).

NUMBERING SYSTEM
See jersey numbers.

NUTCRACKER
A specially designed drill to toughen up players, in which one player is double-teamed with two others. The lone player attempts to get away and the others try to stop him.

O

ODD DEFENCE
A spacing of the defensive line which has players overshifting to one side of the centre. Also called odd spacing.

ODD SPACING
See odd defence.

OFFENCE
The team in possession of the ball.

OFFENSIVE DELAY OF GAME
See delay of game.

OFFENSIVE GUARD
The interior lineman positioned between the centre and tackle on either side of the offensive line of scrimmage.

OFFENSIVE PLAY
A running or passing manoeuvre by the attacking team designed to gain yardage and/or score a touchdown.

OFFENSIVE TACKLE
The interior lineman positioned between the guard and end on either side of the offensive line of scrimmage, sometimes next to a tightend.

OFFENSIVE UNIT
The players on the attacking team.

OFF GUARD
The offensive lineman next to the centre, away from the flow of play. Also called trailing guard.

OFFICIALS
The seven men charged with enforcing game rules and regulating play: referee, umpires, head linesman, line judge, back judge, side judge and field judge.

OFFICIALS' SIGNALS

Football officials use a set of hand and arm signals to inform players, coaches and spectators of the progress of the game. Each signal has a special meaning. For example, when the referee places both hands on his hips and points to one of the teams, this signifies that the team is offside. Raising both arms aloft indicates that a score has been made – a touchdown, a field goal or a conversion.

OFFICIAL TIME OUT

The stopping of the game clock; any of the seven officials may do this, though usually it is the referees, to suspend game action to allow time penalty assessment, conferring, a 2-minute warning, exchange of possession or simply TV commercials.

OFFSIDE

A penalty called against any player who crosses into the neutral zone before the ball is snapped.

OFFSIDE GUARD

See off guard.

OFFSIDE TACKLE

See off tackle.

OFF TACKLE

The offensive lineman between the guard and splitend, away from the flow of play. Also called trailing tackle.

OFF TACKLE SLANT

A running play in which the ballcarrier runs into the line of scrimmage just outside an offensive tackle and between the tightend.

OFF THE BALL
The offensive line charge that takes place at the exact moment the ball is snapped.

OFF TO THE RACES
A long touchdown pass.

OLD LEATHER
A veteran player.

ON-A-ROLL
A team which maintains its momentum while in possession of the ball.

ONE-BACK OFFENCE
An offensive formation which has only one runningback behind the quarterback, plus two tightends and two receivers. Much in vogue in modern pro football and used extensively by the Washington Redskins and the Los Angeles Rams.

ONE-ON-ONE
One offensive and defensive player up against each other.

ON GUARD
The interior lineman positioned next to the centre and on the side of the offensive line where the play is being run. Also called onside guard.

ON SIDE
The part of an offensive formation from the centre to the sideline on the side of the field to which, or on which, a play is being run. Also called spread side.

ONSIDE GUARD
See on guard.

ONSIDE KICK
A strategic manoeuvre by the kick-off team in which the ball is deliberately booted a short distance – a minimum of 10 yards – in order to regain possession, since after 10 yards it is a free ball. This tactic is usually employed late in a close-scoring game.

ONSIDE TACKLE
See on tackle.

ON TACKLE
The interior lineman next to the on guard on the side where a play is being run. Also called onside tackle.

ON THE MONEY
A very accurate pass.

ON THE NUMBERS
A very accurate pass which is thrown and caught chest-high.

OPEN
When a receiver runs a pass pattern and gets away from the defenders, he is said to be wide open.

OPEN END
See splitend.

OPEN FIELD
See downfield.

OPEN SIDE
See on side.

OPEN THE DOOR, KATIE
A very long touchdown pass.

OPTION
In offensive play, where the ballcarrier has the choice of running or passing.

OPTION SPLIT-BLOCK
An offensive manoeuvre in which the splitend has the choice of blocking the cornerback or running a pass pattern.

ORANGE CRUSH
The current Denver Broncos defence.

OUTLAND TROPHY
The annual award for the top college defensive lineman.

OUTLET
The third-choice receiver in a pass pattern.

OUT OF BOUNDS
The area outside the field of play.

OUTSIDE
The area of the field between the offensive tackle or tightend and the sideline.

OUTSIDE SPLIT
A pass pattern in which the back runs at an angle downfield between the safety man and cornerback.

OVER
A pass pattern in which the splitend replaces his block and angles toward the centre of the field at full speed.

OVERSHIFT
See odd defence.

OVER THE TOP
See hi-diddle-diddle.

OVERTIME
Fifteen minutes' extra time made available when teams are tied after the 60 minutes of regulation play. Overtime ends as soon as one team scores. *See also* sudden death.

OWN GOAL
The goal line to be defended.

P

PADS
Foam padding used to protect shoulders, knees, hips and ribs.

PASS
The act of throwing the ball forward of the line of scrimmage from one offensive player to another.

PASSER
The offensive player who throws the football downfield from behind the line of scrimmage.

PASSING DOWN
An offensive play where a pass is anticipated.

PASSING GAME
A game plan which utilizes a lot of passes.

PASSING SITUATION
See passing down.

PASSING TEAM
A team which lives or dies by the passing game, like the San Diego Chargers, Miami Dolphins, Denver Broncos and New York Jets.

PASS PATTERN
A planned, predetermined route run by any one of five eligible pass receivers which will aid the passer in completing a forward pass. Also called pass route.

PASS PREVENT DEFENCE
A defensive alignment in which extra defensive backs are substituted to counter an obvious passing situation.

PASS PROTECTION
Offensive line blocking which protects the passer and allows him to get the ball downfield to a receiver.

PASS ROUTE
See pass pattern.

PASS RUSH
A defensive manoeuvre designed to put pressure on a passer attempting to pass.

PASS TREE
A playbook diagram which shows each eligible pass receiver the pass pattern he should run on a particular pass play.

PAT
Abbreviation for point after touchdown.

PEEL
A player in motion away from the formation.

PEEL BLOCK
Blocking a defender moving back towards the line of scrimmage; used of offensive linemen.

PENALIZE/PENALTY
To enforce the game rules after an infraction by imposing loss of yardage, down loss or other disciplinary action.

PENALTY MARKER
A weighted yellow cloth carried by game officials and thrown to the ground to indicate a rule violation. Also called flag on the play.

PENETRATION
Effective defensive pressure resulting from an aggressive charge across the scrimmage line.

PERIOD
One of the four official 15-minute time segments in a game.

PERSONAL FOUL
An illegal act of aggression by one player against another; for example, unnecessary roughness, clipping, hurdling, piling on, striking with fists, kicking or running into a passer or kicker. Subject to a 15-yard penalty.

PICK
A type of offensive manoeuvre in which linemen switch blocking assignments.

PICK-A-HOLE
A running play in which the back looks for a gap in the line.

PICKET
A protective wall formed by the players on kick-off, and punting teams, to facilitate a successful return by the ballcarrier.

PICK-UP-THE-BLITZ
A blocking assignment for the backfield men to contain or impede linebackers or members of the defensive secondary charging the passer.

PICK OFF

To intercept, as when a defensive player catches a forward pass instead of the offensive pass receiver for whom it was intended.

PIGSKIN

The football.

PILING ON

Deliberately falling on or charging into the ballcarrier or any on-ground player after the ball is whistled dead. This rule infraction is subject to a 15-yard penalty.

PINCHING

A manoeuvre in which two defensive linemen charge from each side of one blocker and catch him between them.

PIT

The area at the line of scrimmage where the offensive linemen and the defensive linemen fight for supremacy.

PITCH

The act of tossing the football underhand to a back moving to the outside of the line of scrimmage, usually on a sweep or a quick pitch.

PITCHOUT

A short pass thrown by the quarterback to a halfback or fullback who is out in the flat zone. Also called a backward pass, shuffle pass or toss.

PLACE KICK

Kicking the ball from a fixed position on the ground, held by a teammate. For the kick-off, the ball may be held or placed on a kicking tee (not over 3 inches in height); a field goal or PAT kicked with the ball held on the ground.

PLACEKICKER

An offensive specialist who takes field goals, PATS and kick-offs.

PLATOON

The offensive or defensive playing unit.

PLAY

A plan of attack by the offensive team which allows it to move the ball down the field.

PLAY ACTION

An offensive play in which the quarterback fakes a hand-off to a runningback, hoping to get the defence to react to a run. Then he passes to a receiver who should be open downfield. Also called a play-number pass or play pass.

PLAY BOOK
A team's reference manual, containing diagrams of various offensive and defensive formations and with each man's assignment clearly indicated.

PLAY FROM SCRIMMAGE
The action started by the snap of the ball.

PLAYING FIELD
See field of play.

PLAY LOOSE
To stay behind and slightly away from the pass receiver as he runs his pattern: a manoeuvre used against extremely fast receivers to prevent long pass completion.

PLAY-NUMBER PASS
See play action.

PLAY-OFFS
A system employed in the National Football League to

determine which teams will progress to the Superbowl. A play-off berth goes to each of the six division winners. The two best teams from the National Football Conference and the American Football Conference then play in a wildcard to decide which two will make up the eight teams for the play-off.

PLAY ON A SHORT FIELD
To have the ball in a good position to start a drive for a touchdown.

PLAY PASS
See play action.

PLAY PROGRESSION
A series of offensive plays, each having the same or similar action.

PLAY TIGHT
To stay as close as possible to the pass receiver as he runs his pattern.

PLUG A HOLE
To fill an opening in the line created by the offence, one in which a defender has previously been knocked aside, thereby stopping the ballcarrier.

PLUGGER
See linebacker.

PLUNGE
A backfield manoeuvre in which the fullback carries the ball into the middle of the offensive line while the quarterback continues to move backward after the hand-off to fullback, and fakes a hand-off to the halfback.

POCKET
See cup.

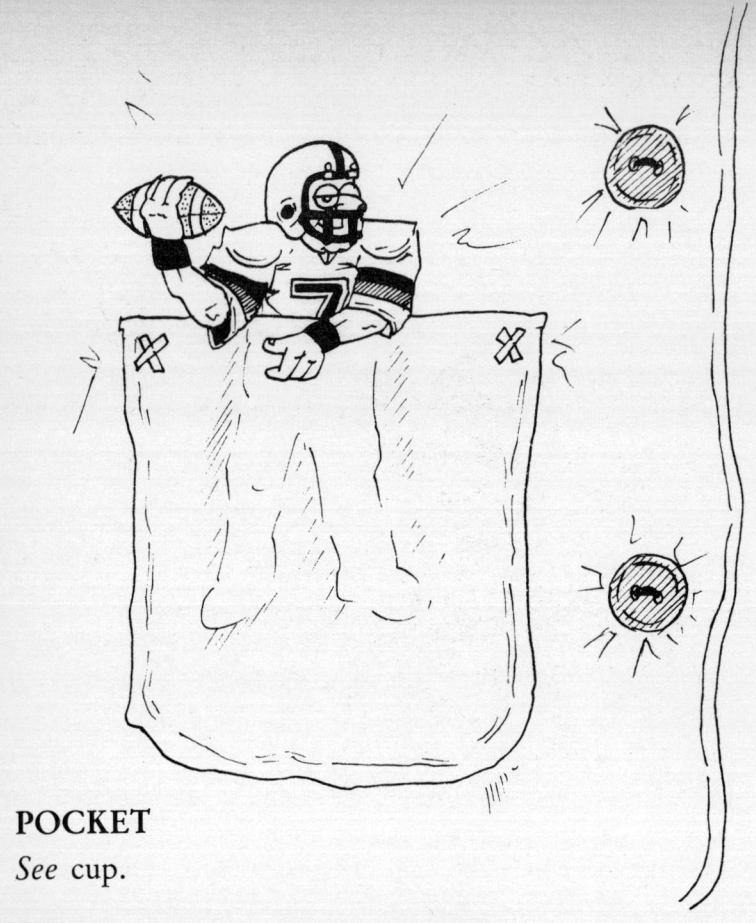

POINT AFTER TOUCHDOWN
See conversion.

POINT OF ATTACK
The designated area where running play will make an impact along the line of scrimmage.

POINT OF FOUL
The exact spot where a rule infraction occurs.

POINT SPREAD
The predicted number of points by which one team will win a specific game.

POOCH PUNT
A soft, delicate, coffin-corner punt, usually from around the 50-yard line.

POP
A pass pattern in which a back moves through an opening in the line of scrimmage and continues into the open area in the centre of the field.

POSSESSION
Control of the football by the offensive team.

POSSESSION PLAY
Third down play.

POSSESSION RECEIVER
A receiver for whom the quarterback will look when a crucial catch is required.

POST PATTERN
A pass route in which the receiver runs downfield, then cuts diagonally towards the goal posts.

POWER BACK
A big runner who picks up yardage because of his size and strength rather than his speed or deception. *See also* bull and horse.

POWER BLOCK
A straight-ahead charge designed to remove a defender from the point of attack.

POWER I
A variation of I-formation in which one offensive back lines up in the traditional position of a T-formation halfback behind the offensive tackle, and the remaining two backs align themselves behind the quarterback in I-formation.

POWER PLAY
Any play in which the set back runs into a given hole before the runningback carrying the ball comes through.

POWER SWEEP
A running play to the outside in which two or more linemen serve as blockers for the ballcarrier. The runner must belly back slightly to allow the offensive linemen to set up a blocking channel before he turns upfield.

PREVENT DEFENCE
Deployment of additional defensive backs in obvious passing situations. *See* dime defence, nickel defence.

PRIMARY RECEIVER
The runningback, wide receiver or tightend to whom the quarterback first looks to throw.

PRO BOWL
The final game of the NFL season, played in Hawaii between the most valuable players of the American Football Conference and the National Football Conference.

PRO FOOTBALL HALL OF FAME
The professional institution in Canton, Ohio, which honours the game's top players, coaches and administrators.

PRO SET
An offensive formation in which two runningbacks line up in the backfield in a variety of positions behind the quarterback. Also called a two-back defence.

PULL
An offensive lineman vacating his spot on the line and moving laterally to lead a block for a runningback.

PULLING GUARD
An offensive lineman who lead-blocks for a ballcarrier.

PULL TAFFY
Repeatedly exchanged possession of the ball that takes place without either team mounting a scoring drive.

PUMP
A simulated throw by a quarterback made to distract the defenders' attention from the direction in which he will throw.

PUNT
To drop the ball from the hands and kick it before it touches the ground.

PUNTER
A player who executes a punt.

PUNT FORMATION
An offensive alignment, usually used on fourth down, with the aim of getting the ball sufficiently far into the opponent's half of the field to start a drive.

PUNT RETURN
The yardage gained following a punt reception.

PUNT RETURN SPECIALIST
A player who receives and returns a punted ball.

PURE
Very skilled in one particular aspect of the game; for example, a quarterback like Dan Marino of the Miami Dolphins who is a very skilled passer but lacks mobility.

PURPLE PEOPLE EATERS
The Minnesota Vikings' defensive unit of the 1960s and 1970s which comprised Carl Eller and Jim Marshall (both defensive ends), Alan Page, Garry Larsen and Doug Sutherland (all defensive tackles).

PURSUIT
An aggressive lateral movement by the defensive team after the ballcarrier, lasting until the play ends and the ball is blown dead.

PUT IT UP
To pass.

PUT THE HAT ON
To hit a ballcarrier very hard. *See* lay the leather.

Q

QUARTER
See period.

QUARTERBACK
An offensive backfield player, set directly behind the centre. He is the 'field general', calling the plays in the huddle. The quarterback is usually the passer, except when he hands-off the ball on an option play.

QUARTERBACK DRAW
An offensive play in which the quarterback steps back from the line of scrimmage with the ball, then quickly moves forward through the line of scrimmage.

QUARTERBACK SACK
See sack.

QUARTERBACK SNEAK

A play in which the quarterback moves straight ahead behind the line charge of centre and guards immediately after taking the snap.

QUICK COUNT

A tactic used by the offensive team to snap the ball on the first sound by the quarterback as he sets up behind the centre, with the aim of surprising the defensive team.

QUICK FEET

Ones which can gather momentum very fast from a standing start. They usually belong to runningbacks. Marcus Allen of the Los Angeles Raiders is a 'quick feet' back.

QUICK HITTER

See quick opener.

QUICK KICK

A surprise offensive manoeuvre in which a backfield man punts the ball from or near his set back position.

QUICK OPENER

A rapidly developing offensive, running play into the line, involving very little deception, in which a back plunges into the hole opened by his blockers. Also called a quick hitter. *See also* quick slant.

QUICK PASS PROTECTION

Pass protection in which the offensive linemen fire out into the defenders head-on in an attempt to get the defenders' arms and hands down; used only when the quarterback is expected to release the ball almost immediately.

QUICK RELEASE

(1) An offensive lineman who brush-blocks a defender, then releases for another block. (2) The ability of a quarterback to set up and throw the ball quickly.

QUICK SLANT

A quick opener in which the runningback runs from an angle usually between the tackle and the tightend.

QUICK STRIKE

A hard, bullet-type pass thrown to a receiver that allows him to catch the ball without breaking stride.

R

RACEHORSE

A receiver who sets the defence problems all the way down the field. His speed does not end a few yards beyond the line of scrimmage but continues like that of a thoroughbred.

RAINBOW

An alley-oops-type pass

RAZZLE-DAZZLE

A surprise offensive play – e.g. a flea-flicker or a reverse – which employs an unusual and unorthodox manoeuvre in order to produce extraordinary results, such as a long gain or a touchdown. Also called trick play.

READING LINE

A defensive line that contains the offence without overwhelming it.

READING LINEMAN

A defender on the line of scimmage who first checks or reads his keys – giveaway signs as to what he is about to do – before charging.

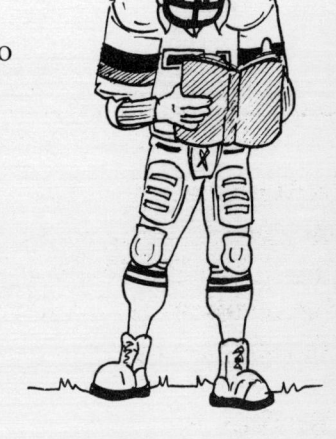

READ PATTERN

A pass play in which the receiver has options on what he does once the play has started.

READ THE DEFENCE

An experienced quarterback will glance at the defence while he is calling the signals and, depending on what he sees (or reads), he may decide to call an audible.

READ THE OFFENCE

To detect the opposition's next move by interpreting its present actions. A clever defensive player can sometimes tell what kind of play the offence will run by 'reading' certain signs; for example, a runningback may indicate the direction of a play by leaning to the right or the left.

READY LIST
A collection of specially designed offensive plays which are to be used against a certain defensive alignment.

RECEIVER
Any offensive player eligible to catch a forward pass, or any player who catches or is designated to catch a punt or kick.

RECEIVING TEAM
The playing unit about to gain possession of the ball from a punt or kick-off.

RECEPTION
The act of catching or gaining possession of a forward pass, punt or kick-off.

RECESS FOOTBALL
Trick plays. *See* Kleenex play, flea-flicker.

RED CHIPPER
A player who is a very good athlete and revels in the big plays.

RED DOG
A defensive play in which a linebacker goes directly after the quarterback. *See also* blitz.

REFEREE
The game's top official. He paces off the penalties, blows

the whistle to signal a dead ball and places the ball at the spot where it will be put in play. Stationed behind the offensive backfield at the start of each play, he is the final authority on the game.

RELEASE
The act of breaking off or freeing oneself from one assignment to perform another; e.g. a tightend blocks first, then goes out for a pass.

REMAINING BACK
The offensive set back who is not carrying the football. Also called a split back or stationary back.

RETURN
The act of advancing a punt, kick or interception. Also called a runback.

REVERSE
An offensive running play in which the quarterback hands-off to a back going in one direction, who then hands-off to a back going in the other direction. If this process is repeated during the same play it is called a double reverse; if it is repeated again it is called a triple reverse.

REVERSE FIELD
To stop and change direction.

REVERSE PIVOT
The motion of a quarterback away from the action in the backfield.

RIDE ACTION
A ploy in the offensive backfield in which the quarter-

back moves a short distance with the runningback who is faking into the line.

RIDE-IN
The tightend blocking a linebacker to the inside.

RIDE-OUT
The tightend blocking a linebacker to the outside.

RIDE THE BENCH
To wait for a chance to play (substitutes sit on a bench on the sidelines in readiness).

RIFLE ARM
A quarterback with a strong throw and quick release. Also called a blacksmith's arm.

RIFLE SHOT
See bullet pass.

RIGHT ON THE MONEY
An extremely accurate pass that drops right into the receiver's hand; also called right on the numbers.

RIGHT ON THE NUMBERS
See right on the money.

RING HIS BELL
To administer a hard hit to another player, usually to the helmet, which causes the victim to hear a ringing noise in his head.

RIVERBOAT GAMBLER
See Mississippi gambler.

ROD
See downbox.

RODMAN
See chain gang.

ROLL OUT
A lateral movement made to either side of the line of scrimmage with the aim of gaining time to throw a forward pass, pitch out or run with the football.

ROLL TO THE SOFT SPOT
To pick the best hole along the line of scrimmage.

ROLL WITH THE BLOCK
To relax or move with the impetus of contact.

ROOKIE
A first-year player in professional football.

ROSTER
The list of players on a team.

ROTATION
The planned adjustment of linebackers and the secondary to meet the strength of certain formations.

ROUGE
A score worth one point in Canadian football only. A kicking team is awarded the point if one of its kicks (a punt or a kick-off) is not returned out of the end zone, which measures 25 yards (US end zones measure 10 yards).

ROUGHING
Illegally hitting a man who is out of the play.

ROUGHING THE KICKER
Illegally contacting the kicker without touching the ball.

ROUGHING THE PASSER
Illegally contacting a passer who has already thrown a pass; subject to a penalty of 15 yards and automatic first down.

ROVERBACK
A middle linebacker.

RULE INFRACTION
See penalty, foul.

RUN AND SHOOT
A pass-happy attack popularized by Moose Davis when he was head coach at Portland State University, the USFL's Houston Gamblers and Denver Gold. It requires the quarterback to roll out to one side of the field and pass on the run. Quarterbacks Neil Lomax (Portland State and St Louis Cardinals) and Jim Kelly (Houston Gamblers and Buffalo Bills) are two of the best exponents of this art.

RUNBACK
See return.

RUNNER
An offensive ballcarrier.

RUNNING BACK
The offensive player who gets the ball on a hand-off

from the quarterback and tries to advance it downfield.

RUNNING GAME
A game which utilizes a lot of running plays.

RUNNING TEAM
An offensive unit which runs effectively with the ball.

RUN OUT THE CLOCK
To protect a lead by utilizing plays that take up a lot of time, usually in the final minutes of a game.

RUN TO THE DAYLIGHT
To run with the ball to an open spot on the field.

RUSH
To charge or run across the line after the ballcarrier or passer.

RUSHING
An offensive; the statistical category for running yardage measured from the line of scrimmage.

S

SACK
The action of tackling a quarterback before he can release a forward pass.

SAFETY
A defensive scoring play in which the offensive player in possession of the ball is tackled or is ruled to be down in his own end zone.

SAFETY SACK
A successful manoeuvre by a deep defensive back in which the quarterback is tackled.

SAFETY VALVE
A short pass thrown to the last open receiver on a quarterback's list. A dump-off pass which gains short yardage.

SAGGING MIDDLE
The weak interior of the offensive or defensive line.

SANDWICH
See double team.

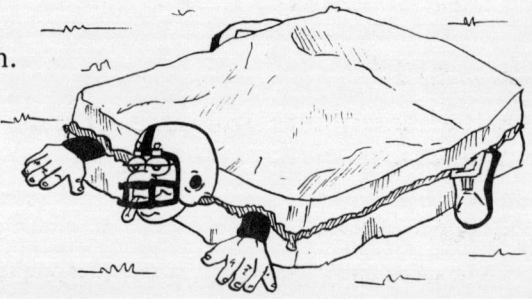

SATELLITE EXPRESS
An offensive formation which takes the term 'pass-happy' to its limits. Three receivers line up on the same

side (a trips or flood formation), one behind the other, like aircraft ready for take-off. The third of these receivers is the triple flanker. There are sometimes four receivers on one side of the field and, on occasion, even five. This game plan was popularized by the Mississippi Valley State University.

SCATBACK
A small, lightweight runningback who relies on speed, deception and quick moves rather than size and power.

SCHOOL'S OUT
A touchdown run.

SCRAMBLE
To move around behind the line of scrimmage in an attempt to elude on-rushing defenders.

SCRAMBLER
A quarterback who is inclined to scramble. Fran 'The Scram' Tarkenton, ex-quarterback of the Minnesota Vikings and the New York Giants, was a master of the art, as are Joe Montana (San Francisco 49ers), Randall Cunningham (Philadelphia Eagles) and John Elway (Denver Broncos).

SCRAPE
A linebacker stunt around a defensive lineman from a stacked formation.

SCREEN PASS
A short pass thrown to a runningback in the flat or to a wide receiver or tightend who has stepped back or remained stationary at the line of scrimmage. To make the screen work, the offensive line will just brush-block

the defensive line before letting them through. The quarterback then throws the ball over the top of the changing defenders.

SCRIMMAGE

Any play beginning with the centre snapping the ball and ending with the official blowing the ball dead. Also an unofficial game or a practice session. *See also* line of scrimmage.

SCRIMMAGE DOWN

Any play which begins when the ball is put into play by a snap from the centre.

SEAL

The act of closing off an area by blocking or channelling the defenders away from the ballcarrier.

SEAM

The undefended area in between two zones of a defensive secondary in zone coverage.

SECONDARY

The cornerbacks and safeties in a defensive backfield. Also the area downfield behind the linebackers.

SECONDARY RECEIVER

The second-choice receiver on any pass play.

SECOND EFFORT

A ballcarrier will sometimes use a sudden burst of energy to gain extra yards when it seems he has been stopped.

SELL-OUT CROWD
A capacity crowd. *See also* blackout.

SERIES OF DOWNS
The permitted four plays from the line of scrimmage which allow the offensive team to gain 10 yards or more in order to retain possession.

SENIOR
A fourth-year high school or college player.

SET
The offensive or defensive formation at the start of every play.

SET BACK
A runningback.

SET UP
To assume a passing position.

SHAKE
A deep pass pattern.

SHANK
To miskick or punt, usually with the side of the foot or ankle.

SHIFT
To change position before the start of a play.

SHIVER
The thrusting of the forearm, on the part of a defensive lineman, into the upper body of the offensive lineman in order to deflect his block.

SHOESTRING CATCH
To catch the pass just above the ground.

SHOESTRING TACKLE
A tackle born of desperation in which the defender just manages to get his hands around the foot or ankle of the ballcarrier.

SHOOT
A defensive change from either the linebacker or the secondary position.

SHOOT-OUT
A high-scoring game. The San Diego Chargers' offence under coach Don Coryell has been involved in an inordinate number of these.

SHOOT THE GAP
Linebackers or a defensive secondary charging through a hole in the offensive line to the passer or ballcarrier.

SHORT SIDE
The area of the field between the centre and the sideline which has the fewest offensive linemen.

SHORT SQUARE OUT
A pass pattern in which the receiver moves downfield 7 yards, then breaks towards the sideline.

SHORT YARDAGE DEFENCE
Using extra defensive linemen and linebackers to stop an anticipated running play when the offence needs just a few yards to keep a drive alive or score a touchdown.

SHORT YARDAGE OFFENCE
Using extra blockers (tightends, tackles or powerful fullbacks) when just a few yards are needed to keep a drive alive or score a touchdown.

SHOTGUN
A passing formation in which the quarterback sets 4-5 yards behind the centre with other backfield men split out as flankers or slotbacks; popularized in 1975 by the Dallas Cowboys and now used by several other professional teams.

SHOULDER POP
Contacting a defender by driving the shoulder into his body.

SHOVE PASS
See shuffle pass.

SHUFFLE PASS
An underhand pass. A toss, pitchout or lateral pass. Also called a shove pass.

SHUT OUT

To play a game without allowing your opponent to score while your team scores; to blank the other team.

SIDE JUDGE

A game official, positioned 17 yards downfield from the line of scrimmage, whose responsibilities include assessing the legality of receptions, pass interference, downfield blocks and clipping on punt returns.

SIDELINE-AND-GO

A pass pattern in which the receiver cuts to the outside, then heads straight downfield at full speed. Also called a sideline take-off.

SIDELINE PATTERN

A pass pattern in which the receiver runs to the outside towards the sideline.

SIDELINE TAKE-OFF

See sideline-and-go.

SIDELINES

The parallel lines running the length of the field which mark the designated boundaries of the playing field.

SIDE ZONE
One of two areas on the field of play which are 23½ yards wide and 100 yards long and are bounded by the goal lines, inbound line and sideline.

SINGLE COVERAGE
A defensive back who covers the receiver by himself.

SINGLE WING
An offensive formation characterized by the fullback (tailback) lining up 5 yards behind the middle of the offensive line and the quarterback (blocking back) standing one yard behind the line half-way between the centre and the end, while the halfback (wingback) lines up outside the strong-side end. This formation is no longer used in modern professional football.

SIXTY-MINUTE MAN
A very durable player.

SLAM
Making a hard shoulder block on a defender and then withdrawing to carry out another assignment.

SLANT
A running play in which the ballcarrier takes the handoff and runs at an angle through the line of scrimmage. Also a pass pattern in which the receiver moves 3 yards straight across the line of scrimmage, then breaks towards the inside.

SLANT PASS
A pass pattern in which the receiver runs up to 15 yards downfield and slants in towards the middle of the field. Also called an inside slip.

SLED
Training apparatus consisting of a steel frame and large cylinders used by players to practise blocking and tackling.

SLOPPY BLOCK
Offensive line blocking which allows the lineman to get in position for a screen pass.

SLOT
The area in the offensive backfield between the tightend and the tackle.

SLOTBACK
A receiver set up behind the line of scrimmage between the tightend and the tackle.

SNAKE IN
A pass pattern in which the receiver moves downfield, then circles toward the inside.

SNAKE OUT
A pass pattern in which the receiver moves downfield, then circles toward the outside.

SNAPPING THE BALL
A backward pass by the centre, through his legs, to start a play. Also called a hike.

SNEAK RECEIVER

A pass receiver who blocks or delays, then runs the pass pattern close to the line of scrimmage away from the flow of play.

SOFT HANDS

Those of a very good receiver.

SOFT PASS

A lightly thrown football. *See* feather the ball.

SOPHOMORE

A second-year high school or college player.

SOPHOMORE JINX

A second-year professional player who after a brilliant start to his career hits a slump, leaving observers to conclude that he was just a flash in the pan.

SPEARING

To dive head-first into an opponent who is already on the ground; subject to a 15-yard penalty and automatic first down.

SPECIAL TEAMS
The playing unit used in any kicking situation.

SPIKE
To throw the ball straight down in the end zone after scoring a touchdown.

SPIRAL
A smoothly rotating ball which has been passed or kicked.

SPLIT
The gap between two offensive linemen.

SPLIT BACKS
Two offensive players in a tight backfield who line up in halfback positions. *See also* set backs, remaining backs.

SPLITEND
The receiver stationed furthest away from the tackle. Also called the open end.

SPLIT LINE
The line spacing between guards and tackles determined by the play call.

SPLIT THE UPRIGHTS
To kick a field goal or PAT conversion right in the middle of the goal posts.

SPOT
A quick pass thrown to a receiver moving straight across the line of scrimmage.

SPOT OF ENFORCEMENT
The point from which a penalty is marked off.

SPOTTER
A member of the radio or television broadcast team who identifies players for the play-by-play man.

SPREAD ENDS
See split end.

SPREAD SIDE
See on side.

SQUARE IN

A pass pattern in which the receiver runs downfield for 10-15 yards and then cuts to the inside.

SQUARE OUT

A pass pattern in which the receiver runs downfield for 10-15 yards and then cuts to the outside.

SQUARE OUT AND DOWN

See fly pattern.

SQUEEZE

Double team blocking by the offensive guard and tackle on a defensive lineman.

STACK DEFENCE

A 4-3 defence in which the linebackers set up directly behind the down linemen.

STANDARD NUMBERING SYSTEM
See jersey numbers.

STATIONARY BACK
See remaining back.

STATUE OF LIBERTY
An offensive play characterized by the quarterback taking several steps back with the ball, raising his arms as if to pass, then handing off to the backfield man who has run behind him. Once popular with collegians; rarely seen today in pro football.

STAY IN YOUR LANE
An instruction given to members of the kick-off team so that they can converge on the returner.

STEM
To change the defensive alignment just before the snap.

STICKUM
An illegal adhesive substance once used by pass receivers or defensive backs to aid ball-catching. Lester Hayes and Fred Bilitnekoff of the Los Angeles Raiders were the most famous users of stickum.

STIFF ARM
See straight arm.

STRAIGHT ARM
A rigid extension of the arm in an effort to ward off a tackler. Also called stiff arm.

STREAK
A pass pattern in which the receiver runs straight downfield at full speed with no fakes.

STRIKING
Swinging, clubbing or propelling the arm or forearm when contacting an opponent.

STRING IT OUT
To extend a lateral running play as far as possible toward the sidelines before trying to turn it upfield.

STRIPPING THE BALL
Trying to take the ball away from the ballcarrier by forcing him to fumble the ball.

STRONG SAFETY
The defensive back who lines up in the defensive secondary on the same side as the tightend.

STRONG SIDE
The side of an offensive alignment in which the tightend is positioned.

STUDENT BODY RIGHT
The sweep as run by the University of Southern California Trojans' Marcus Allen (now with the Los Angeles Raiders), who made this play his own and ran up 2,342 yards in his final collegiate year to win the Heisman Trophy in 1981.

STUNT
Altering the defensive line charge to attack the ballcarrier from an unusual angle.

STUNTING
Moving in and out of the defensive line to confuse the offensive team.

STUTTER STEP
A faking movement by a ballcarrier, trying to elude tacklers by making short, chopping movements. Also called a juke step.

SUBMARINE
Lunging forward as close to the ground as possible to tackle a ballcarrier, usually around the ankle.

SUDDEN DEATH
The result gained during a 15-minute time extension granted when teams have tied. The first team to score a touchdown, field goal or safety will be the winner. In championships or play-offs the overtime period may be extended indefinitely until a result is secured.

SUICIDE SQUAD
A special team of players used on kick-offs, punts, field goals and PATs. They are usually rookies or substitutes who are trying to impress the coaches. *See also* bomb squad and kicking unit.

SUPERBOWL

The championship final of the National Football League, which is played in January every year. Heralded by probably the biggest media hype of any sporting event, it brings together the champions of the NFC and the AFC to compete for the Vince Lombardi trophy. The first Superbowl, played in 1967, resulted from the merger of the NFL and the American Football League.

SUSPENDED PLAYER

One who is withdrawn, for at least one down, to remove illegal equipment.

SWEEP

See end sweep and student body right.

SWIM

A technique, resembling that of a freestyle swimmer, used by defensive linemen or a tightend to get by an opponent.

SWING PASS

A pass pattern in which the remaining back runs around the defensive end on the same side. *See* flare pass.

SWIRL

A pass pattern in which a wide receiver or tightend begins to run a crossing route, stops, then turns to run back to the outside.

SWIVEL HIPS

A shifty, elusive ballcarrier who fakes potential tacklers by shifting his hips from side to side.

T

TACKLE
(1) An offensive lineman positioned between a guard and a tightend. A defensive lineman positioned between an end and another tackle. (2) To stop a ballcarrier's progress by seizing and overpowering him, then dragging him to the ground.

TACKLE-ELIGIBLE
To be able, in certain situations, legally to operate as a tightend or receiver; used of offensive linemen.

TACKLING DUMMY
A heavy, foam-filled bag used to simulate a ballcarrier for tackling practice.

TAILBACK
An offensive backfield man in single-wing formation positioned 5 yards behind the line of scrimmage almost directly behind the centre.

TAKE A SHOT
Make an attempt.

TAKE AWAY/GIVE AWAY
To take the ball away from the other team by way of interception or fumble; to give the ball to the team by way of interception or fumble.

TANK
A big, powerful runningback who is very hard to stop. *See also* bull and horse.

TAXI SQUAD
Players under contract who practise with the team but are not included in the official team roster and do not take part in league games. If a player on the team is injured, a taxi-squad member is activated to take his place. The term derives from the one-time owner of the Cleveland Browns, Mickey McBride, the owner of a fleet of cabs. In the 1940s, players who were not good enough to make the Browns were given the job of driving one of McBride's cabs to keep them available in case of injury or other problems.

TD
Abbreviation for touchdown.

TEE
See kicking tee.

T-FORMATION
An offensive alignment in which the quarterback lines up directly behind the centre, with a fullback a few yards behind him set between two halfbacks. Also called a basic T or tight T.

THAT'S ALL, SHE WROTE
A touchdown run.

THREE-FOUR DEFENCE
A defensive formation with three down linemen at the line of scrimmage and four linebackers.

THREE-POINT STANCE
The basic football stance, in which a player crouches with his legs apart and one hand touching the ground in front of him.

THROW INTO A CROWD/TRAFFIC
To pass into a group of potential receivers and potential interceptors where the chance of any offensive player being able to catch the ball is slim. *See also* forcing the ball and throw it away.

THROW IT AWAY
To pass the ball safely out of the reach of any defender when all of your potential receivers are covered. The exact opposite of throwing into a crowd/traffic.

THROW THE ROCK
A hard, bullet-type pass.

TIGHTEND
A pass receiver positioned near the tackle, whose basic assignments are blocking and running short-pass patterns.

TIGHT SAFETY
The defensive back who covers the tightend on pass plays: usually a strong safety.

TIGHT T
See T-formation, basic T.

TIME IN
The point at which a play has officially started following a time out, initiated by a back judge who restarts his watch.

TIME OUT
An interval during the game when play, and the clock, stop. This occurs in the following situations: (1) when

the ball goes out of bounds; (2) after a fair catch reception; (3) when the ball goes dead; (4) at the end of a down when a foul occurs; (5) after an incomplete pass; (6) at the signal of 2 minutes remaining in the half and in the game; (7) at the end of a period; (8) when a ball is illegally touched or recovered; (9) during a change of possession; (10) when a team requests it.

TIMING PATTERN
A specially designed pass route in which a quarterback throws to a certain spot on the field at a certain time in synchronization with a wide receiver.

TIP-OFF
Any idiosyncrasy of an offensive player which might tell the defensive player where the play is going. Also called a key.

TOSS
See shuffle pass.

TOUCHBACK
When a ball is downed in the end zone by the receiving team following a kick-off, punt, interception or fumble, that team gets possession of the ball at its 20-yard line.

TOUCHDOWN
The primary objective of the game. Six points are awarded for carrying the ball across the goal line or receiving a pass in the end zone.

TOUCH FOOTBALL
An inexpensive and enjoyable type of football which can be played on any open plot of land by 2-11 players. The

ballcarrier is stopped by being touched by an opposing player, so the game relies a lot on passing.

TRAIL
A pass pattern in which a receiver runs downfield 10 yards, then squares in.

TRAILING GUARD
See off guard.

TRAILING TACKLE
See off tackle.

TRAINER
The person responsible for assisting in the treatment of injured players during games, training camp and practice sessions.

TRAP BLOCK
The act of blocking an unsuspecting, defensive lineman, usually from the side, after he has penetrated the line of scrimmage. The offensive lineman will allow his opponent to come across the line of scrimmage, then block out to the side, so that the ballcarrier can charge through the area left open by the defensive player.

TRENCHES
The area around the line of scrimmage in which offensive and defensive linemen fight for supremacy. The side which wins this battle will probably dominate the game.

TRICK PLAY
See razzle-dazzle.

TRIPLE FLANKER
See satellite express.

TRIPLE OPTION
A play in which the quarterback hands-off to a back straight up the middle, pitches out to a back on a sweep or runs the ball himself; used mostly in college football.

TRIPLE REVERSE
See reverse.

TRIPLE-THREAT BACK
An offensive back (usually a runningback) who can run well with the football, pass on occasion and kick (or punt). Slinging Sammy Baugh, a quarterback with the Washington Redskins in the 1930s, was the last big triple-threat back. Today a triple-threat back is one who runs exceptionally well, can pass and is a good receiver, since all teams now have a specialist punter or kicker. Runningbacks are rarely, if ever, required to punt or kick. Two of today's versions of the triple-threat backs are Marcus Allen (Los Angeles Raiders) and Walter Payton (Chicago Bears).

TRIPS FORMATION
See satellite express.

TRY FOR POINT
See conversion.

TURK, THE
The most dreaded person in pro football. He is responsible for telling a player that his career with that particular team is over. The name alludes to a Middle-Eastern warrior wielding his scimitar.

TURN-AND-GO
See hook-and-go.

TURN BLOCK
Contact by a tightend with the first man to his outside.

TURN IN
A pass pattern in which the receiver runs a few yards downfield and then cuts straight across toward the middle of the field.

TURN IT OVER
To punt the ball slowly end over end, giving the kick more distance and making it more difficult for the punt returner to catch it.

TURN OUT
A pass pattern in which the receiver runs downfield at three-quarter speed, changes to full speed, loops to the outside, then turns back toward the quarterback.

TURN OUT AND IN
A pass pattern in which the receiver moves straight downfield, fakes to the outside, then moves to the inside, running parallel to the line of scrimmage.

TURN OUT THE LIGHTS
A touchdown run.

TURNOVER
A fumble recovery, pass interception, blocked punt or field goal.

TURN THE CORNER
To run laterally then turn upfield.

TWIST
An offensive blocking manoeuvre in which linemen exchange blocking assignments.

TWO-BACK OFFENCE
See pro set.

TWO-MINUTE DRILL
See hurry-up offence.

TWO-MINUTE WARNING
The referee's message to each head coach that 2 minutes are left in the half – and in the game.

TWO-ON-ONE
See double team.

TWO-POINT STANCE
The basic football stance, but without the player's hand touching the ground.

TWO-WAY PLAYER
Any player who plays both ways. In the past, when there was a roster limitation, this was very common. Nowadays, however, every position is highly specialized and two-way players are very rare. The most recent example is Roy Green of the St Louis Cardinals, who was drafted as a defensive back but now plays wide receiver. He was the last player to make a reception and an interception in the same game.

U

UMPIRE
An official who has primary jurisdiction over the equipment, conduct and action of the players on the scrimmage line. He assists the referee in decisions involving possession of ball in close proximity of the line and races on offensive linemen moving downfield in a passing situation.

UNBALANCED LINE
An unusual offensive formation in which the offensive lineman lines up one side of the centre. So instead of a centre with a guard and a tackle on either side plus a tightend, the formation has a centre and a tackle on one side plus two guards, a tackle and a tightend on the other side.

UNDERNEATH
The area between the defensive backs and linebackers.

UNDERSHIFT
A defensive line movement toward the weak side of an offensive formation to confuse blocking assignments; a manoeuvre deployed to thwart anticipated running play to the weak side of the formation.

UNDER-THE-CENTRE
The position of the quarterback crouching behind the centre, ready to receive the snap to start a play.

UNIFORM
Jersey, pants, helmet and socks worn by each player.

UNIT
Any team of eleven players, either offensive or defensive, or special teams, e.g. kicking unit, field goal unit or punting unit.

UNSPORTSMANLIKE BEHAVIOUR
Unacceptable or illegal acts by a player which are contrary to the generally understood principles of conduct on field.

UP
In an emotionally charged state before a game.

UPRIGHTS
See goal posts.

V

V-OUT
A pass pattern in which the receiver moves downfield, cuts at an angle to the inside and crosses paths with another receiver, then cuts back to the outside.

VARIATION
A pass or running play in which one or more men alter their usual assignments.

VEER OFFENSIVE
A triple-option offence invented by Bill Yeoman, head coach of the University of Houston Cougars. It is used mainly in colleges and high schools and is meant to help

a team which does not have big, blocking linemen. It is usually run from the I-formation and allows the quarterback to make up his mind once the ball has been snapped.

VERTICAL PASSING GAME
A game plan which calls for a lot of passing. Of the teams which use this, the most famous are the Miami Dolphins, San Diego Chargers and Denver Broncos.

VETERAN
A National Football League player who has played more than one season.

VICE
See double team.

VICTORY DEFENCE
A prevent defence.

W

WAFFLE
A very hard block or tackle.

WAIVER
A player whose services are no longer required by his present team and is traded to another team, or whose services are made available if other teams require them.

WALK-ON
A college player who does not get a football scholarship but who tries out for the team and makes it by hard work and tenacity.

WALK THE TIGHTROPE
The tightrope is another term for the sideline. Receivers 'walk the tightrope' if they catch the ball close to the sideline and tiptoe down that sideline before their momentum carries them out of bounds.

WAVE, THE
A spectator phenomenon invented in the mid-1960s by Rob Weller, then head cheerleader of the University of Washington: spectators stand up and sit down in sections, which when viewed from the field or from the opposite side of the stadium looks like a breaking wave.

WEAK SIDE
The side of the formation away from the receiver and tightend.

WEDGE
A formation used on kick-off returns in which players line up shoulder to shoulder in front of the ballcarrier to block for him.

WEDGE BLOCK
To form a moving V-shaped protective force in punt or kick-off return plays.

WEDGEBREAKER
A member of the kick-off team assigned to knock down or separate a wedge formed by the return team.

WIDE RECEIVER
A flanker or splitend set furthest away from the tightend or weak side tackle.

WIDE SIDE
The area between the ball and the sideline furthest from the ball.

WILDCARD

A team which makes the pro play-offs without finishing in its division. The NFL awards four wildcards each season. They go to the two teams with the best records in each conference which did not win their division titles.

WINGBACK

A runningback in a single wing formation who lines up outside the strong side tightend.

WISHBONE

A triple-option offence pioneered by Darrell Royal when head coach at the University of Texas. It uses three runningbacks in the backfield, one behind the quarterback and one behind each of the offensive guards. It gives the quarterback the option of handing-off, passing or running with the ball himself.

X

X
Legend used in coaching diagrams for splitend receiver or tightend.

Y

Y
Legend used in coaching diagrams for the tightend.

YARDAGE
The distance gained or lost on a play from scrimmage; yards gained by the team with the ball.

YARDAGE CHAIN
See chain.

YARDLINE
The markings on the field of play in 5- and 10-yard increments from goal to goal.

YARDSTICKS
The vertical poles attached to the yardage chain, used to mark the point where the down series began and a point 10 yards away.

Z

Z

Legend used on coaching diagrams for flanker.

ZEBRA

A nickname for a game official – derived from their black-and-white-striped shirts.

ZIG-IN

A pass pattern in which an eligible receiver runs downfield 10 yards, takes a step to the inside, cuts diagonally to the outside for 3-5 yards, then cuts back again to the inside.

ZIG-OUT

A pass pattern in which the eligible receiver runs downfield 10 yards, takes a step to the outside, cuts diagonally inside for 3-5 yards, then cuts back again toward the outside.

Z-IN

See zig-in.

Z-OUT

See zig-out.

ZONE

A pass defence in which each player is responsible for one area on the field and is not specifically assigned to cover a man.

ZONE BLOCKING
See area block.

ZONE COVERAGE
See zone defence.

ZONE DEFENCE
A pass prevent deployment in which defenders cover assigned areas of field rather than individual pass receivers. Also called zone coverage.

RADCLIFFE PHILLIPS, the author, was one of the founder members of the American Football League in Britain and founder and owner of the Milton Keynes, Bucks team. The first full-time commissioner for American football for any European country, he is on the board of directors of the European Football League, has coached both adults and juniors and founded the Milton Keynes Yearlings, Britain's first junior team. He is now head coach with the Coventry Bears in the Budweiser Premier Division. Radcliffe Phillips has reviewed American football on an informal basis for various publications and is the editor of the *British American Football Rule Book* (Columbus Books).

DAVID TIDSWELL, the illustrator, lives and works in Nottingham as a civil servant. A part-time illustrator with his own small studio, he plays tightend for the Nottingham Hoods and first met Radcliffe Phillips when the latter was commissioner of the British American Football League.

Also published by Columbus Books

THE BRITISH AMERICAN FOOTBALL RULE BOOK
Edited by Radcliffe Phillips

The rules of British American football are based on those of the National Collegiate Athletic Association in America, on which all American football rules are based.

This rule book contains:
- full diagram of the playing field
- at-a-glance summary of penalties
- 44 illustrated officials' signals
- penalties and signals for North American players
- in-depth explanation of each individual rule
- complete list of British teams.